REAL WOMEN.
REAL STORIES.

MIKVAH STORIES

A Collection of True Stories of Women
Overcoming Today's Challenges

COMPILED BY CHAYA RAICHIK

First published 2022
Copyright © 2022 by Chaya Raichik
ISBN: 978-1-56871-691-6

Published by
Targum Publishers
Shlomo ben Yosef 131a/1
Jerusalem 9380581
editor@targumpublishers.com

For more information visit www.mikvahstories.com or
email hello@mikvahstories.com.

For book copies and bulk orders email orders@mikvahstories.com

Cover design by Esty Raskin.

B"H

Dedicated to all Jewish women everywhere.

May they receive abundant blessings of
sholom bayis,
nachas from children,
prosperity,
good health,
and the strength to overcome life's challenges.

Just like the *mesiras nefesh* for *Taharas Hamishpacha*
brought about our redemption from *Mitzrayim,*
may the extra efforts we make
for the observance of *Taharas Hamishpacha*
bring *Moshiach* now.

Acknowledgments

I would like to start off by thanking *Hashem* for giving me the merit to be able to publish a book on such an important topic. It's an honor and a privilege to be the messenger.

I would also like to acknowledge all the *brachos* from the *Lubavitcher Rebbe*, strongly encouraging the writing of a book and not to delay in writing it.

Thank you (in no particular order) to:

- My aunt, Devorie Wilhelm for believing in me and giving me my first leads.
- Nechama Prus for getting the ball rolling.
- Chani Carlebach, Goldie Plotkin, Rivky Slonim and Sarah Karmely for their help .
- All of the wonderful women who gave of their time to share their personal stories in the hopes of inspiring and encouraging other women to be strong for this foundational *mitzvah*.
- The Union Street *mikvah*.
- Akiva Atwood and the staff at Targum Press for turning my dream into a reality.
- Chassi Rivkin of www.mikvah.org for their contributions to the book. (Check out their website – it has tons of info, resources, and valuable information!)
- Sara Esther Crispe for her edits and feedback. (Just one more story!)
- Chava Dumas for the initial editing.

- Esty Raskin for all the graphic design and for your endless patience, positivity and knowledge. What would I do without you? Instagram is @estyraskin.
- Mimi Kulek for your help way back when I was starting out.
- Aimee Baron of #Iwassuppossedtohaveababy.
- Mrs. Esther Piekarski for her help and her insight on *niddah* from the "Bodies and Souls" podcast by Rivky Boyarsky and Sara Loewenthal.
- Mrs. Sara Morozow
- Dr. Yael Mayefsky
- Sara Blau of EmBRace Magazine.
- Altie Raskin for your leads.
- Yettel Zylbernagel, Leah Abraham and Aviva Guerevitch for listening to my ideas and providing feedback.
- Chaya Zirkind and the Sheuir Group for boosts of energy
- The "East Flatbush Past the Hospital Side" community for being the best support group. Rabbi Yossi tells us in *Pirkei Avos* that the best thing for a person to have is a good neighbor and we are so lucky to have a whole community of good neighbors!
- Estie Shurpin for her writing skills. This book would not have happened without her wit, wisdom and talent. She took the words that I gave her and turned them into enchanting stories; stories that one is drawn to read and to be inspired.
- My wonderful, amazing sisters-in-law Rishi, Chana'le, Hindy, Chaya Mushka and Hindy. Thank you Rishi and Hindy for your invaluable advice!
- My sisters, Chana and Breindel. Thank you best stenographer Chana for your excellent proofreading and late nights adding oxford commas, removing cop out? cop-out? hyphens, and overall pedantic grammar. (Should've had you review this)
- My mother and mother-in-law for their encouragement and for reading way too many versions.
- My kids for their wonder for life and teaching me new things every day.
- My husband for supporting me through all the story collecting and decisions; editing and re-editing; and for making it all possible.

Disclaimers

The compiler spent many years painstankingly collecting stories. She went to great lengths to personally verify each story. Each modern-day story was shared first hand by the woman involved in the story and was shared with permission. Some details may have been changed to keep the stories anonymous or for clarity. Dialogue may have been added or embelished. The author and publisher assume no responsibilities for any mistakes or innacuracies and hereby disclaim any party for any damage caused by any errors for any cause.

Please do not interpret halacha, Jewish law, from any of these stories. Each woman and situation is unique, and an Orthodox Rabbi must be consulted if there are any questions.

This book isn't meant to give advice about mental health or shalom bayis. Relationships are complex. The purpose of this book is to inspire women to be more aware and more careful of their Taharas Hamishpacha observance. The mitzvah of Taharas Hamishpacha brings brachos of shalom bayis and children to a home. For some situations, adding in this mitzvah will be enough while other situations will call for the advice of a Rav, Mashpia and/or therapist.

This is meant to be a light read, to reawaken the spark of joy and holiness, and to help women "fall in love again" with the mitzvah of mikvah.

Haskamos

23 Adar 5781

I applaud Mrs. Chaya Mushka Raichik's efforts in collecting and documenting inspirational *mikvah* related stories.

Each anecdote provides insight, perspective, and *chizuk* for women to enhance their observance of the holy *mitzvah* of *Taharas Hamishpacha*. The variety of locations and types of women interviewed, as well as the diverse incidents described, would make such a book "something for everyone", very relatable to many audiences.

Sara Morozow
Veteran *kallah* teacher
Crown Heights, NY

Haskamos

26 Adar 5781

This book is spellbinding! Your depiction of dedication to the *mitzvah* of *mikvah*, the yearning people feel, and the lengths to which they will go to bring *hidur mitzvah*, to elevate this commandment, brings the experience to a higher and holier level. *Mikvah Stories* is so moving and inspiring that even readers who may not be obligated to use the *mikvah* will be motivated to elevate their observance of other *mitzvot*.

Miryam Yerushalmi,
Counselor, motivational speaker, and
author of "*Heavenly Waters: Mikvah Meditations*"
and the "*Reaching New Heights*" series

Why I Wrote this Book:

Doesn't every woman have a *mikvah* story (only one?!)?

Going to the *mikvah* is one of the more private aspects of Jewish observance giving it the opportunity to be exciting and dramatic. Whether you're taking a taxi up the main Jewish avenue to get to the *mikvah* before *Shabbos* while ducking your head and praying you don't see anyone you know, or making a *bedikah* in the strangest of places (summer trip to the zoo?), following the *halachos* of *Taharas Hamishpacha*[1] gives us Jewish women plenty of opportunity for stories. From the new *Rebbetzin's mikvah* night falling out on *Yom Kippur* to the *hefsek tahara* needing to be made on the same day as your best friend's wedding, *Taharas Hamishpacha* can be an exciting *mitzvah*.

Taharas Hamishpacha can also be challenging; the more important the *mitzvah* is, the more the *Yetzer Hora*[2] tries to stop us. The purpose of this book is to find yourself in one of these stories and to gain the strength to overcome your own challenge(s), whatever they may be. Learn from the women in these stories, regular woman in today's times, and be inspired!

This book has a diverse collection of stories from women of all different ages and stages in life, women of all different backgrounds and experiences, each with their own voice. This book wasn't written for one specific type of woman either. My hope is that each reader

---

1 Lit "Laws of family purity". This refers to the collection of laws regarding marriage, intimacy, preparing for and using the *mikvah*.
2 Evil inclination

can find at least one or two stories to relate to, to connect to, to think about, and draw strength from at the right time.

Compiling the stories for this book was eye-opening. It was inspiring to hear stories from so many women, modern- day heroines, who overcame various challenges in order to go to *mikvah* in the best possible way.

Yet it's important to keep in mind that the *mitzvah* of being intimate only while in a state of purity is so fundamental, that there are *poskim* who maintain that *yaharog v'al yavor*, a person should let themselves be killed rather than transgress. A community is also obligated to sell their *shul* and *sifrei torah* if they need funds to build a *mikvah*. The stories in this book are meant to be inspiring and thought-provoking, yet at the same time, we keep the vital *mitzvos* of *Taharas Hamishpacha* even when we are not inspired, simply because *Hashem* told us to.

In this book, there are quite a few stories of women that conceived children after making the extra effort for *mikvah*. The *Lubavitcher Rebbe* said many times that a woman who wants to conceive children or have more *nachas* from her current children, should make an extra effort to be more careful in areas related to the home; such as being more careful with covering her hair, more stringent in observing the laws of *Taharas Hamishpacha*, and making an extra effort for *sholom bayis* in the home.

That being said, we do not know the ways of *Hashem*. It says in *Sifsei Chachamim* on Rashi[3], that *Sara Immainu* and *Rivka Immainu* merited to have the cloud of the *Shechina* above their tent from week to week as a symbol of their meticulous observance of *Taharas Hamishpacha*. However, *Sara Immainu* and *Rivka Immainu* both waited many years before they conceived. Clearly, their *Taharas Hamishpacha* observance was scrupulous and *Hashem* wanted them to remain childless for other reasons.

Our role as Jewish women is to be careful in our observance of *Taharas Hamishpacha*, while leaving the rest up to *Hashem*. May this in itself be a merit for us to receive the great *brachos* of children and *nachas* from our children.

This book is for you, dear reader, in whatever stage of Jewish

---

3   Beraishis, Perek Chof Daled, Pasuk Samach Zayin, Sifsei Chachamim 40

observance you consider yourself. Whether you're a newbie or a *mikvah* pro, this book is for you to read, to laugh, to cry, to grow, to empower yourself, and become more connected to yourself, *Hashem*, and the *mikvah*.

Kosher!
Chaya Mushka Raichik
Chof Beis Shvat 5781

Preface:
Why is Taharas Hamishpacha So Important?

The *halachos* of *Taharas Hamishpacha*, or "the Laws of Family Purity," encompass one of the most fundamental *mitzvos*. The entire Jewish family life revolves around these *halachos*.

Sometimes there are misconceptions about these *halachos*, with purity being erroneously translated as "clean" and impure being translated as the opposite of clean. Nothing could be further from the truth. Going to *mikvah* is not about becoming "clean", it's about becoming pure and holy. The concept of purity is completely spiritual; it's a dichotomy that *Hashem* invented and only He understands. It's a part of Jewish life that we follow simply because He said so.

An impurity is explained as a lack in one's regular spiritual connection to *Hashem*. Similar to the gaps in a ladder, the time of impurity allows one to pause and refresh before continuing up the next rung and deepening the connection with *Hashem*.

Nowadays, most of the laws of purity and impurity don't apply because we don't have the *Beis Hamikdash* and therefore we are all in various states of impurity. Only a woman who is immersing in the *mikvah* to be able to be intimate with her husband after a *niddah* period receives this unique opportunity to refresh her connection with *Hashem* in the modern era.

Carefully following the *halachos* of Taharas Hamishpacha has positive spiritual, physical and emotional effects on intimacy and a child yet-to-be conceived. Therefore, the entire future of the Jewish people rests on proper usage of the *mikvah*. This is a weighty responsibility given solely to Jewish women who have proved time and time again their tremendous dedication and commitment to fulfilling this properly.

We can further understand this by taking some lessons from the story of *Chanukah*.

When learning about *Chanukah*, we mostly hear the stories of the small band of brave Maccabees fighting against the massive and advantaged Greek army, or of how the pure jar of olive oil miraculously remained lit in the Menorah for eight days. Less known is the role of Jewish women in the *Chanukah* story. In fact, the Jewish woman is so central to the *Chanukah* story, that women have a custom to refrain from doing any work during the time that the candles are lit each night. But what was so special about the women's role?

The entire focus of Greek culture at that time was to secularize the Jews. Initially, they only forbade the practice of several "irrational *mitzvos*" including *Taharas Hamishpacha*, *Bris Milah*, and some others. The Greeks denied that holiness, spirituality, and purity exist. They insisted that everything must be logical and understood by the human mind.

The Greeks had a rule that before any Jewish bride would marry, she first needed to spend the night with the Greek ruler of her town. The Greeks wanted to show that marriage isn't holy and there is no deep significance to being intimate other than having a good time (similar ideas are prevalent in our society now).

In contrast, the Torah says that a woman is valued and holy. Women are not objects. The Torah declares that intimacy is sacred and women are sacred. Intimacy is a time of mutual, shared connection and is to be reserved for marriage and even then, not at all times. Intimacy is for when a woman is emotionally, mentally and spiritually ready as per the *halachos* of *Taharas Hamishpacha*. She willfully consents, they are not angry at each other, and she has undergone a proper immersion.

After the Greeks made this decree, the Jewish community tried to evade it through different tactics, such as changing the day they customarily got married. When it was the turn of Yehudis[4], a relative of Mattisyahu *Kohen Gadol*, the High Priest, to get married, she was forcibly brought before Helifornos, the general of her town. She gave him strong cheese and wine to get him drunk and then cut off his head. This, together with the mobilization of Mattisyahu and his five sons, drove fear into the Greek soldiers of the town, and they fled. This was the beginning of the band of Maccabees, the war for the heart and soul of *Yiddishkeit*, and the fight for holiness and purity. This is what ultimately led to the miracles of *Chanukah*. The entire holiday of *Chanukah* came about because of the *mesiras nefesh* of one woman for *Taharas Hamishpacha*, for purity and holiness!

Continuing further in the story, when the Maccabees dedicated the Menorah in the *Beis Hamikdash*, they insisted on only using pure olive oil that hadn't become impure in any way. Although it was a state of emergency and they could have used regular olive oil, the Maccabees wanted to show *Hashem* that they had completely won over the Greeks; that holiness and purity had won and they would only use pure olive oil for the Menorah. In return, *Hashem* made a miracle that caused the oil in the Menorah to burn for eight days and nights while messengers were sent to get new pure olive oil.

With the lessons of *Chanukah* in mind, we can understand the importance and significance of becoming pure by following the *halachos* of *Taharas Hamishpacha* and using the *mikvah*. This is not something rational, rather it's a reflection of our connection to *Hashem*; an unbreakable, suprarational connection, not defined by logic or understanding.

---

4   There are several different variations of the story. The way it is presented here is according to the opinion of the *Ran*.

Contents

Why I Wrote This Book: 10

Preface: Why is *Taharas Hamishpacha*
so Important?..13

Story One Under Fire...21

Story Two When You Help Others, Hashem Helps You 24

Story Three Focus 26

Story Four An Enchanting *Mikvah* Journey...........29

Story Five *Mikvah* Will Carry You Through........33

Story Six Snowstorm!..36

Story Seven Siberia in Canada 38

Story Eight Inspiration...40

Story Nine Nailed It 42

Story Ten For the Sake of a *Mitzvah*...................43

Story Eleven A Little Nudge 46

Story Twelve His Mother's Lasting Impact 48

Story Thirteen Overcoming My Water Phobia.........50

Story Fourteen Do Something Extra 53

Story Fifteen *Segulot v'Matanot!*.........................55

Story Sixteen Just in Time 60

Story Seventeen Determined....................................63

Story Eighteen An Unexpected Benefit................................65

Story Nineteen The Final Immersion 67

Story Twenty The Right Decision 70

Story Twenty-One Surrender................................72

Story Twenty-Two His Different Plan................................75

Story Twenty-Three *Chafifah* Preparation at the Airport? 77

Story Twenty-Four Just Do It 80

Story Twenty-Five *Mesiras Nefesh* American-Style................81

Story Twenty-Six You Never Know................................83

Story Twenty-Seven Nuuu...? 84

Story Twenty-Eight An Elevated *Mikvah* Story.................. 87

Story Twenty-Nine Pop!................................89

Story Thirty Why *Mikvah*?................................ 91

Story Thirty-One "Of Course!"................................ 97

Story Thirty-Two My *Mikvah* Experience 99

Story Thirty-Three *Taharas Hamishpacha* Saves Lives...........102

Story Thirty-Four The *Mitzvah* That Kept on Giving............104

Story Thirty-Five A Cross-Country *Mikvah* 107

Story Thirty-Six Musings from Main Street 109

Story Thirty-Seven A Light in the Darkness 111

Story Thirty-Eight Cold? What Cold? 113

Story Thirty-Nine Not Obsessed................................115

Story Forty Still Grateful a Decade Later................118

Story Forty-One Blizzard! 121

Story Forty-Two *Mikvah* and OCD 123

Story Forty-Three *Mikvah* During the COVID-19 Pandemic One 128

Story Forty-Four *Mikvah* During the COVID-19 Pandemic Two................................130

Story Forty-Five *Mikvah* During the COVID-19 Pandemic Three 132

Contents   19

Story Forty-Six *Mikvah* During the COVID-19 Pandemic
Four 134

Story Forty-Seven Real Women, Real *Mesiras Nefesh* 136

Mikvah-Related OCD and How to Help 137

Resources 142

Glossary 144

Biography 150

Story One
Under Fire

It was December of 2008 and my husband and I were living in Be'er Sheva. I had just given birth to our second child. In that month alone, over 600 rockets and mortars were launched by Palestinian terrorists from Gaza into Israel, with Beersheva a primary target. This was before the Iron Dome technology had been developed, and residents were urged to stay within range of a bomb shelter at all times. In fact, only medical personnel were allowed on the street. We were on high alert, as any moment the siren announcing an approaching rocket could go off, and we would have ten seconds to run to the bomb shelter before the BOOM as the rocket hit. It was a dangerous and scary time.

Several weeks after my baby was born, I faced a difficult dilemma. I wanted to go to the *mikvah*, but it wouldn't be simple or safe. During a time of peace, I would have had many *mikvahs* to choose from. The *mikvahs* are spread out all over the city, throughout the nine different neighborhoods, tucked away in corners and at the end of winding paths. Having many different options allowed for privacy on *mikvah* night even in my sociable Israeli community. However, at that point, only one *mikvah* in the entire city of Beersheva was open for use; the only one the *Rabbonim* deemed safe. Obviously, it wasn't very private, and I wasn't thrilled with the idea of meeting the whole city at the *mikvah*. Nonetheless, that wasn't my primary concern by far. I was much more worried about my own and my family's safety.

In our very tight knit Moroccan community, everyone was talking about was how dangerous it was. Everyone wanted to know what people were going to do about going to the *mikvah*.

I was torn. On the one hand going to the *mikvah* was extremely scary. We were living in a war zone, and our home was not one with easy access to a regular bomb shelter. The safest place in our house was the stairwell. When the sirens would sound, we would run there with our children to wait for the all clear. The thought of leaving my husband alone with our two kids, one of them a newborn, was terrifying. Getting to the *mikvah* would also be an ordeal, as traveling anywhere on the open roads meant putting oneself in danger. Just the thought of traveling alone at night was unsettling.

On the other hand, I knew the significance of using the *mikvah*, the many *brachos* it brought to the family, and its importance for *shalom bayis*[5]. Furthermore, I had learned that one is protected when doing something holy such as attending the *mikvah*. I realized that while some people might have said forget it in this kind of situation, for me it wasn't so much a question of *if* I would go, as much as *how* I would go.

The evening I spent preparing for the *mikvah* was extremely stressful. I was so worried about leaving my family and going out on the road, that I could barely focus on the task at hand. I kept second-guessing my decision to go.

With trembling fingers, I called a taxi and waited with trepidation for it to arrive. After what felt like an eternity, a driver finally pulled up outside our home. I climbed in and gave the driver, who appeared completely secular, the address of my destination. "Oh," he said, with obvious recognition, "The *mikvah*!" I felt so uncomfortable at that moment, and I simply didn't know what to do with myself. The driver didn't miss a beat, "Where do you think I am going every night? I'm taking women to the *mikvah*! And don't worry," he continued, "I'll even wait for you!"

I was so overcome with relief; I didn't know whether to laugh or to cry. I felt so thankful to *Hashem* that this wonderful man should be the taxi driver that showed up at my door on that stressful night, with just the right words to reassure me that I had made the right decision;

---

5   Lit, "peace in the home". This common phrase is used in many different contexts to refer to a harmonious, loving relationship between husband and wife.

and the promise that he would wait to make sure that I would return home safely. I can still see the taxi driver's face in the mirror all these years later, and I still laugh with a mixture of humor and relief whenever I tell the story. It was an extremely difficult decision to leave my family and go out in a time of danger, but *Hashem* sent me a *malach* that night to make sure I made it to the *mikvah* and back, safe and sound.

Story Two

When You Help Others, Hashem Helps You

During my residency in medical school, my schedule was particularly grueling. I was spending long hours at the hospital, and every fourth night I had an overnight shift. One winter afternoon was particularly difficult. I was ready to go to the *mikvah* that night, which, in the city where I was living, required a pre-scheduled appointment. The *mikvah* would only open if it was requested and only at the specific time you arranged.

I had scheduled an appointment and was planning on going right after my shift at the hospital. In the late afternoon, a patient under my care "coded" and required CPR. As the managing resident, I was swept into a storm of in-the-moment decisions as we fought to stabilize the patient. I managed to find a moment to do the last *bedikah* while I was relieved for a quick break. As my shift wound down and the patient still wasn't stable, I found myself struggling to hand over care to the incoming resident. Even though my shift was technically over, I wanted to give the best care that I could, and I wasn't looking at the clock.

By the time I was able to leave the hospital, it was already 9:00 P.M. I immediately called the *mikvah*, but I found that it was closed. I was devastated. Pushing it off for the next night wasn't practical since I was scheduled for one of my overnight shifts, and I was crushed at the thought of going home to my waiting husband and telling him that it hadn't worked out. I wasn't a doctor and I couldn't make my own hours yet, so between the overnight shifts and the late-night hours, I had hardly been around the last few months.

Unsure of how to proceed, I decided to reach out to a friend for the *mikvah* attendant's private phone number. I'm not sure what I expected, but I called and explained what had happened and asked if there was any way I could still come to the *mikvah* that night. This was no small request since I still had to prepare and the *mikvah* attendant was less than thrilled that she'd opened the *mikvah* earlier, and I had turned out to be a no-show.

For a moment, there was silence on the other end, and then the *mikvah* attendant said "You know, I closed the *mikvah* over an hour ago, but *shalom bayis* is important, and taking care of patients is also important. I'll open for you again."

I was so grateful to *Hashem* that the *mikvah* lady agreed to help me and come back to the *mikvah* she had already closed. I realized at that moment that sometimes it is important to reach out and ask for help, and that when you help others, *Hashem* helps you.

It definitely wasn't simple or easy, but I made it to the *mikvah* that night!

Story Three
Focus

Not again.

No.

I just don't want to go. I'm not ready.

It was the night before I was scheduled to go to the *mikvah* after having my third child, just three and a half years after my marriage.

I was tired. So tired. My pregnancy had been full of children climbing on me; during the day by the preschoolers I was teaching, and during the evenings, by my own children. After birth, I was attached to my newborn, his tiny mouth constantly crying out for me, wanting to suck.

My body just wanted a break. My arms. My lap. My toes. I just wanted my body all to myself. I wanted to feel like a person again, and I just was not ready to share.

But how long could I push it off for already? The weeks were ticking by, and I felt bad for my husband who was patiently waiting. So I began my *mikvah* preparations and hoped that when it was time to go, I would be excited again.

But now it was the night before, and I was dreading it completely. Deep down inside, I wanted it to feel special. I wanted to connect with my husband after all those weeks of waiting. I wanted it to go well. So I woke up the next morning with a purpose. I was going to make it work.

After dropping off my two older ones at the babysitter, I headed with the baby to an upscale spa some distance away. A thoughtful neighbor had gifted me a baby present of a gift certificate towards a manicure at this spa and I decided that this was a good opportunity.

On the way, I decided I needed some inspiration, and I went to mikvah.org's website where I found a speech discussing the beauty of *mikvah* night. I found myself soaking up the words as I listened to the speaker's passionate, empowering speech. As I walked along, pushing my stroller in one hand and fiddling with my headphones with the other, I found myself tearing up. Oh, how I so badly wanted to have a rejuvenating *mikvah* night!

It was a long lecture and I listened throughout my manicure. There was still plenty left to listen to later that night as I was doing my preparations in the *mikvah* room. I thought about her words of how *mikvah* night was a time of connection, how *mikvah* night was a time for us to make each other happy, a time to rediscover our relationship. And it resonated.

I realized that *mikvah* night was only going to be amazing if I did the work. So as I clipped my toenails, I thought of how special my husband was. Clip. He noticed I was so tired last week and offered to wash the dishes. Clip. Clip. He was still changing the baby's diapers when he was around. Clip. He offered to do the laundry. Clip. Clip. And so on. I was determined that this *mikvah* night was going to be all the wonderful things the lecture spoke about.

As each part to prepare came up, something funny happened. Suddenly my body was different. My mouth was sparkling clean. Nothing stuck between my teeth. My hands? No traces of the colorful marker and sharpie stains that had been my trademark during the time I was teaching. My legs? Had a good shave for the first time in a long while. Each part of me just tumbled into the next as I reclaimed my body. My arms were mine again, the toenails that I could finally reach again to cut, they were mine again. My whole body was mine again. As I checked myself in the mirror for my final inspection, a shiver of anticipation raced through me. This was my body and I was ready.

I put on my robe, called for the attendant, and went to the *mikvah* room. As I started down the steps, I could feel the waters beckoning to me. A strong feeling came over me and I could feel the holiness in the room. I slowly dipped beneath the waters and as they came gushing over me, a wave of deep emotion also rushed over me, into me, and around me, spilling out of me. It was a feeling so strong that I just could not contain it. At that moment, I was unified with my Creator. The deepest parts of me had merged with my Creator.

I had won. I had worked all day on developing my relationship with the *mikvah*, *Hashem*, and my husband and I had won.

I made the *brachah* and dipped several more times, *davening* from my depths to continue to have *sholom bayis and* to feel connected to my husband.

As I stepped out of the *mikvah* and put on my robe, touching the hand of the *mikvah* attendant, I could not shake the feeling. It was still a part of me and I knew that this was the *Shechinah* of *Hashem,* the Divine Presence, resting within me. It stayed with me as I dressed up and put on my makeup. I took stock of myself in the mirror, enjoying my reflection and turned to go.

I was ready.

Story Four
An Enchanting Mikvah Journey

It was nine years ago, but this story is etched in my mind forever. Why? Because I see it in front of me every single beautiful day.

I was not *frum* by any means; I was actually quite the rebel growing up. At the age of forty-three I decided to leave a high paying job with all the social benefits that it came with. At the same time, I started to become *Shomer Shabbat*, but that was the extent of my becoming religious. I started to work for an organization called JEP: Jewish Experiences Program. A very kind and intelligent rabbi ran it together with his wife.

They approached me one day and offered to give me a generous stipend for new clothing so I could buy skirts and dresses that would be more appropriate for my new work environment. I accepted, and that was the beginning of the most beautiful life that awaited me.

Once I started wearing skirts and shells to work, I rarely dressed any other way nights or weekends. I was in charge of marketing a Torah class for *frum* women regarding *Taharas Hamishpacha*[6] given in a home in a religious neighborhood.

I only went to the class to collect the money and take attendance.

The women were seated in the dining room around a table, and the *Rabbanit* sat at the head of the table. I sat down only to collect and write down the names of those who attended. As I got up to leave, I worried it would be disruptive, so I waited for the right opportunity to leave. Little did I know I would be drawn in, pulled like a magnet,

6   The collection of laws related to Family Purity and immersing in the *mikvah*

and the two hours sped by like a minute. I was left thirsty for more. There was so much I didn't know about the *mikvah*, the preparations and the laws. They were so intricate yet so fascinating.

I listened to every morsel of wisdom coming out of this wonderful, knowledgeable *Rabbanit*. She was so beautiful, elegant, and inspirational! All the women were taking down notes, which was foreign to me having left school so long ago. Later on, I realized the importance of taking down notes at any class you attend. But this one even more so, since you need to look back and review the notes practically every month, especially at the beginning when it's not automatic and you don't know much.

I went to the second and third class, absolutely loved it, and made friends with the women there. They all thought I was *frum* like they were because of how I dressed. But I had never gone to a *mikvah* once, not even before my wedding.

When winter break came and there was still one class left to go, my husband and I went away for a week to Mexico. Before we left for our trip, I had finished being *niddah* and I decided I wanted to do all of the preparations for *mikvah*, as I had learned in the classes, and immerse while in Mexico. After counting five days of separation, I started counting the seven days of purity and checking myself with the special *bedikah* cloths that I had bought. I checked every evening and every morning trying to do every single detail to perfection.

On our third day in Mexico, it was time for me to go to the *mikvah* for my first time. We took a taxi there and my husband waited outside. it was the most beautiful sensual sensation, and I felt so close to *Hashem*. I felt so privileged, I felt young, vibrant, and felt wanted by my husband waiting outside.

I took my time getting ready. The *mikvah* was small, very old fashioned, but so romantic with pink walls and low lights, a beautiful oasis. Once I was ready, a woman came to get me. As we walked to the *mikvah* together, I felt like I was being led like a queen, an empress, ready to dip in this delicious warm water. This pure sanctified water. As I immersed, I felt tears of joy run down my cheeks; at 47 years old I was given the chance to experience the bliss of an intimate, spiritual bond with my husband, one that celebrated me as his wife, to the exclusion of all others. I felt so pure and so valued.

When I said the *brachah*, which I repeated after the woman, I felt I was saying this prayer directly to *Hashem*. It was my first real connection with my Creator. I felt so solemn, but I also felt a peace and tranquility and an assurance that everything I was doing was right. It was unbelievable.

I got out of the water and was attended to by the *mikvah* attendant like a princess. I was given towels and a *bracha*. I got dressed and went outside to find my husband elated to have his beautiful wife available again. We hugged and kissed as if it were our first time. It was so special to finally hold hands and feel the warmth and comfort of his arms around me. We felt like two kids laughing and walking together. We sat on a terrace and ordered drinks, and my husband was looking at me as if it was our first date. We were so hungry to be together, we didn't stop holding hands and talked so much and laughed. I couldn't have asked for a better vacation.

Meanwhile, I had been hoping to get pregnant for five years. My daughter was about to turn six, and I didn't want there to be such a huge gap, but at my age it didn't come easy. Months prior to this, I had gone to see a specialist to see what was wrong. He looked at me and said, "You're a religious woman?" I said, "Yes," he said, "Then start praying." I had left his office devastated. That was his way of saying that at my age, there was not much to do.

Upon my return home from our vacation in Mexico, the class was to reconvene a couple of weeks later when everyone was back and we all had settled in. By that time, six weeks passed, and when I attended the last class, I had the most beautiful, amazing news even though it was too early for me to share with anyone! *Baruch Hashem*[7], after all those years of wanting and yearning for a baby, I was finally pregnant!

My pregnancy was the best pregnancy ever; I loved every single minute as if it were my first. I was radiant. At my age, at 47, I was pregnant!

I gave birth to the most gorgeous baby girl you have ever seen. Everyone that saw her was struck by her beauty, *Baruch Hashem*. One woman told me something that stuck with me forever, she said that my daughter looked like she was traced by *Hashem*.

I have since been going to *mikvah* religiously and only wished I had

---

7   Thank G-d!

started sooner. I never want it to end. I love being *niddah*, and being careful that my husband doesn't see me with my hair uncovered. That we don't touch by mistake, counting the days, the excitement, learning to love everything about your partner without touching, only with words, and then the day of *mikvah*, the adrenaline between us. It's beautiful. It's very well thought out, and only *Hashem* could make two people feel like a brand-new renewal every month. It's so beautiful; I hope I can go many more years. I wish it would never end!

Story Five
Mikvah will Carry you Through

Oren and Tal* were a young Israeli couple who sent their daughter to our school. While they had been careful with *Taharas Hamishpacha* and *mikvah* in *Eretz Yisrael*, in America things had become lax. While they showed up frequently at our events and our *Shabbos* table, I never saw her at the *mikvah*.

When Tal became pregnant, they were very excited. However, their excitement soon turned to fear and tension when the baby was diagnosed in utero with a genetic abnormality. The couple was distraught and sought my husband's and my support and guidance.

Tal unburdened herself to me, crying that she was overwhelmed and didn't know what to do. She was alone in the United States without family support, and she wasn't sure she wanted to carry the pregnancy to term.

"Listen to me," I told her, "You need to go to the *mikvah*. You need to have five days of separation, count seven clean days and you need to go, and you need to think good thoughts, and it will be good."

Tal agreed and we began to count her days together, but when *mikvah* night came she pushed it off. And then she pushed it off again. Every night there was another reason and another excuse. She was very reluctant, saying, "It's just not a good time." I reminded her frequently, and encouraged her to make the effort, telling her "This *mitzvah* is so powerful, and so many *brachos* come to your family through it."

Finally, after a follow up scan which revealed multiple abnormalities, including one the doctors said might not be consistent with life, Tal counted her days and came to the *mikvah*.

Tal called me a week later to share the news that her next scan showed an entirely different story. The doctors were much more positive in their reports, and they no longer saw many of the problems that had concerned them so greatly at the earlier scan. "Oh Tal, that's wonderful!" I exclaimed. "You just need to keep thinking good thoughts, and everything will be good."

Tal continued to call with updates, informing me of different interventions the doctors were suggesting, and I continued to encourage her to think positively. "The *mitzvah* of *mikvah* will carry you through this, " I told her.

When the baby was born prematurely, Tal called me, crying. The doctors were ready with a list of things that could potentially go wrong, especially following the worrisome scans. The constant stream of possible problems was doubly overwhelming to a newly and unexpectedly postpartum mother. Her tiny preemie felt like a massive weight that she and Oren would have to carry alone.

Again I encouraged her to think good thoughts, and encouraged her to come to the *mikvah*. After each appointment with a specialist, she would call me and I would remind her, "Think good and it will be good. The *mitzvah* of *mikvah* will carry you through."

After a few weeks, the baby was still not improving in the hospital, and Tal called me, upset. "We are thinking good, " she cried. "Why isn't it good?"

"We'll *daven* for her." I said. "What's her Jewish name?" But Oren and Tal hadn't given her a name at the Torah!

"With the older kids and work and the baby in the hospital, it's too hard to get to *shul*." Oren explained. "When things calm down, we can make a *kiddush* and give her a name then."

My husband put his foot down. "She needs a Jewish name. Just tell us what it is and we will name her. You don't need to be there!"

The baby was named the next day; immediately after her naming, she began to improve. She was soon able to go home from the hospital, and a few weeks later, Tal came to the *mikvah* again.

In the end, none of the doctors' dire predictions came to fruition. Oren and Tal's daughter is completely healthy! A beautiful little girl, she attends our school just like her siblings, and her mother comes regularly to the *mikvah*. When I ask how her youngest is doing, she smiles a broad smile. "Good, *Baruch Hashem!* The *mitzvah* of *mikvah* carried us through."

Story Six
Snowstorm!

It was a Thursday in November, and it was snowing softly as I settled into my seat on a New Jersey Transit train. I was headed to Manhattan for a routine appointment and I planned to be back home within a few hours. The following day was my son's *Bar Mitzvah* and I would be hosting lots of family over *Shabbos*. I was also planning to go to the *mikvah* that night.

Exiting the subway station in Manhattan, I noticed that the snow seemed to be coming down a bit harder. Traffic was moving more slowly than usual, and it took me a few extra minutes to navigate the slippery streets. In the back of my mind, I recalculated my (already overfilled) schedule for the day. Accounting for the snow, I mentally added extra time to my trip home and cut out an errand so I would have time to prepare for the *mikvah*.

By the time I left my appointment, the entire world was white. Snow was falling heavily and the wind was blowing fiercely. I could barely see a few feet ahead to navigate back to the subway station. Traffic was moving at a snail's pace and pedestrians like me were few and far between (in Manhattan!). The steps into the subway station were treacherous, slippery, and covered with snow. When I finally reached the platform, my relief quickly became distress. The station was mobbed, trains weren't running, and it was getting late. Recalculating my schedule again, I quickly texted my husband, "Stuck waiting for the train. Pizza for dinner."

After that there was nothing to do but wait.

Afternoon became evening and evening stretched into nighttime. More and more stranded commuters filled the station as the work day ended, seeking shelter from the snow and hopeful that they would soon get home. We all languished on the train platform as the hours passed with no trains (but unfortunately many rats) in sight. After what felt like a lifetime, trains finally started running around 11:00 P.M. Exhausted, freezing and relived, I finally reached home at about a quarter to one in the morning.

But, I still needed to go to the *mikvah*. I loathed putting it off, especially since the next day would be busy preparing for *Shabbos*; full of cooking, family and last-minute preparation for the *Bar Mitzvah*.

I decided I would try to get to the *mikvah* that night. I messaged the *mikvah* attendant, who was definitely not interested in going out in the middle of a blizzard, but after some negotiating, she agreed to give me the keys to the *mikvah*. Now I just needed to find an attendant. Who could I ask to come with me to the *mikvah* at two in the morning?

Suddenly I had an idea. My mother is a night owl, always busy well into the night and often still awake at 2:00 or 3:00 A.M. While a bit uncomfortable, I decided to give it a try and ask her if she'd come with me. After a few (rather awkward) texts back and forth, we agreed to meet on a street corner a few blocks away.

Bundled in layers of sweaters, coats, and scarves we made our way through the deserted, snow-covered streets to the *mikvah*, where I prepared and then immersed in the (thankfully heated!) water.

Our walk back was just as cold and snowy, but I felt warm inside, having made the extra effort for this beautiful *mitzvah*.

Story Seven
Siberia in Canada

Many years ago, I taught the laws of *Taharas Hamishpacha* to a young bride who was not yet observant. We studied the relevant laws and I shared some inspiring stories about the importance and power of the *mikvah*. The story that stood out most was the one about my own grandmother back in Russia, during the freezing Siberian winter. She refused to get married without this important *mitzvah* of immersing in the *mikvah*. She had to break the ice on the surface of a frozen *mikvah* on the night of her own wedding!

The young bride was amazed that someone had had so much self-sacrifice for the *mitzvah*. "Today's *mikvahs* are well maintained, beautifully decorated, and heated!" I told her. "If my grandmother could break the ice, surely you can take on this *mitzvah*."

The young bride was very inspired and, together with her fiancé, decided to commit to keeping the *mitzvah* of *Taharas Hamishpachah*.

I watched the young couple slowly become more observant until, they moved to a small town in Canada a few years after their marriage to further their schooling. While there were *Chabad Shluchim* serving the community, there was no local *mikvah*. Unaware of this, the young woman called the local *Shlucha* a few weeks after their arrival and told her that she needed to use the *mikvah*.

The *Shlucha* was incredulous. "Are you joking?"

She laughed, "There's no *mikvah* here, only students! The closest *mikvah* is several hours away."

"Several hours?" It was the young woman's turn to be incredulous.

"It's the middle of summer in Canada! Sunset is so late. I won't get home until 2:00 A.M.!" She paused for a moment and then asked, "Is there a lake or river nearby that I could use?"

The *Shlucha* was a bit taken aback. "A lake or river? Are you sure? That's a bit scary." But the young woman was certain, so the *Rebbetzin* called a friend who owned a private lakefront cottage. After explaining the situation, and with the permission of the *Rav*, it was arranged to use the lake as a *mikvah* that week.

Even in the summertime, the lake water was chilly, and the late hour only made it colder. The young woman surprised the *Shlucha* when she immersed in the cold lake without so much as a whimper. After making sure she was wrapped warmly in a robe and towel, the *Shlucha* asked her, "How were you able to do this? First, to even think of using a lake, and then to immerse so stoically, without any reaction to the cold water?"

The young woman replied, "Because of the story that I heard from my *kallah* teacher." She then proceeded to tell the *Shlucha* the story of my grandmother breaking the ice to use the *mikvah* on her wedding night in Communist Russia.

The next morning the *Shlucha* called me to tell me what had happened. "Look at this self-sacrifice for *mikvah*," she exclaimed. "It's the strength and commitment of an immersion in Siberia, right here in a small college town in Canada!"

The year and location may change, but the stories of Jewish women's unfailing commitment to this beautiful *mitzvah* are timeless.

Story Eight
Inspiration

In the early 60s, in the middle of the Cold War, we were sent by the *Lubavitcher Rebbe* on a trip to Russia. We thought we were going to inspire and uplift the Jews living behind the Iron Curtain, but really it was quite the reverse. Their dedication and resolve to live a Torah-true life in the face of immense difficulties, inspired and uplifted us tremendously.

While we were there, I was taken on a clandestine tour of the *mikvah*. The woman who showed me around was so proud that they had a *mikvah*, but I was shocked at how primitive it was! The *bor* (pool) where the water collected was simply a concrete pit filled with unfiltered water, heated by a metal rod which needed to be held in the water by hand. The metal would glow red hot and heat the water around it. This heating method was not the most successful to say the least, and women often immersed in cold water.

My tour guide told me with pride how so many women remained connected to the *mitzvah* of *mikvah* even during those difficult times. They were persecuted by the government and often made fun of by their family for keeping this "backwards" tradition, yet they persisted and came to the *mikvah*. Let me tell you, it wasn't a spa!

When I came back to the United States, I arranged a meeting with the ladies of my community. I wanted to share the details of my experience while they were still fresh in my mind so I could accurately describe the self-sacrifice I had seen from our fellow Jews, especially for the *mitzvah* of *mikvah*.

At the meeting, there was one woman in particular who had resisted all of my previous attempts to discuss the *halachos* of *Taharas Hamishpacha*. She just didn't want to hear about the *mitzvah*'s meaning or value, though she wasn't hostile or angry. She was simply indifferent. The *mitzvah* didn't fit in with her lifestyle, and she wanted nothing of it.

I was surprised to see her great interest in the stories I shared about the women I had met, the descriptions of their struggles, and what they endured for the *mitzvah* of *mikvah*. I was even more surprised, shocked really, when she shared her thoughts.

"If they can do it there," she said "under such terrible conditions and with so much danger, then I can do it too." And right then and there, this newly-inspired woman promised to keep the *mitzvos* of *Taharas Hamishpacha* for the rest of her life.

Story Nine
Nailed It

The woman in the preparation room knocked tentatively on the door a few minutes after entering. She looked panic-stricken as she told me that while preparing for the *mikvah*, one of her fake nails had come loose and fallen off. While *tevilah* with fake nails can be kosher in some certain circumstances, if one is cracked or missing, they are all considered a *chatzitza*[8] and one cannot immerse.

Explaining this aspect of Jewish law to the woman before me was no simple feat. The *mikvah* that night was stressful enough for her as it was. Having just experienced a miscarriage in her ongoing attempts to become pregnant, she struggled to take yet another setback in stride.

"I understand that this is a real *nisayon* for you," I said, gently. "Actually, the Hebrew word *nisayon* means both 'test' and 'uplift'. May this difficult test be an opportunity for you to further elevate your *mitzvah*."

I was truly amazed by what followed. For the next hour, this woman sat and painstakingly removed the remaining nine fake nails, taking care that absolutely no residue remained so that her *tevilah* would be kosher.

I embraced her as she left the *mikvah* and told her how incredible and inspiring her dedication to the *mikvah* was.

Ten months later we embraced again when she came to use the *mikvah* after the birth of a healthy baby.

---

8   An obstruction. When immersing in the *mikvah*, there may not be anything extra on the body that can obstruct the *mikvah* waters from flowing and touching the entire person.

Story Ten
For the Sake of a Mitzvah

It had been five long years of marriage and we had not yet been blessed with children. During that time, I watched my brother get married followed by two of my husband's sisters. As the years went by, I watched each of them start growing their families, while my nest was empty.

One year, we traveled to spend *Pesach* with my husband's family. My husband is from a poor second world country and his family lived a 15-minute drive from the *frum* area and the *mikvah*. Despite the poverty and crime going on in the neighborhood, the *mikvah* is beautiful, and I had many pleasant experiences there.

This time, my *mikvah* night fell out on the eighth night of *Pesach*, *Acharon Shel Pesach*. I had always been scrupulous about going to *mikvah* on time, and I was hoping that being careful to go on time, on *Yom Tov*, despite the long walk and the sketchy neighborhoods, would be a merit for us.

I called the *mikvah* attendant who was in charge of the *Shabbos* and *Yom Tov* appointments and we arranged an appointment at 6:45 p.m. She warned me that she would wait for me just until 7:00 p.m and if I didn't show up during that time, then she would go home.

On *Yom Tov* afternoon, I walked together with my husband to the *frum* area. During our hour walk, we passed by many different people in some very dangerous neighborhoods, but I was steadfast in my resolve to *toivel* on time. I dropped my husband off at the *shul*, where I did my final *bedikah* and headed several blocks over to the heavily gated and guarded *mikvah*.

When I arrived, the guard nodded and let me in. I waited and waited and waited. It was 6:55 and the *mikvah* lady had not shown up. The guard felt bad for me and asked if I was sure the attendant was going to meet me. I told him that I had made an appointment. He suggested that I try to go to her house, but I had no idea who she was or where she lived.

A few minutes later it started pouring rain, my watch turned 7:00 and I just cried.

It was too much. I was in the rain, outside a *mikvah*, in a foreign and unsafe area, protected by a non-Jewish guard, and I had such a strong desire to fulfill this *mitzvah*.

The guard felt terrible. He told me that he knows where the *mikvah* attendant lives, but he doesn't know her address. If I hid in the guard booth under the desk out of sight, then he would run to her house to get her.

I agreed.

After what felt like forever, I heard a woman's voice and the voice of the guard. I came out of the booth and a woman in a snood, started shouting her apologies to me. She had simply forgotten. We went into the *mikvah* and she ushered me into the preparation room.

I had never been so relieved to dip in the *mikvah*. I always felt connected to the rebirth concept that *mikvah* provides. It is usually a time of deep, spiritual connection for me; a time when I daven for children and *brachos*. This time, I just felt relief and prayed silently as I heard the woman's voice and the ticking of the clock.

I met my husband outside. He asked me if I was OK and what took so long? And for the hour and fifteen minutes that we walked home in the pouring rain, I retold my story. I was so sure this would be it. This would be my *mikvah* story. I would retell it and add the postscript that *Baruch Hashem*, a year later we were blessed with a child. I felt the *mesiras nefesh* as we walked through the sketchy neighborhoods soaked to the bone and came home to the meal almost two hours late. I thought this is going to be my story.

And it is.

Except two weeks later, just after accompanying my younger sister-in-law Mindy to the *mikvah*, I went home to discover that right on time, my period had come.

I understood that I was not given the reward I had felt so deserving of.

It hurt.

I thought back to all the stories I had heard of, all the times that women had *mesiras nefesh* and merited to conceive a child, and for the second time that month I cried.

I cried and I cried and then I sat down and thought.

I thought about what *mikvah* really means to me and what *mikvah* means to *Hashem*. At what point had I connected being scrupulous about all the details to specific *brachos*? When did I make the switch from *mikvah* being a time of rebirth and spirituality to it being about my fertility status? I realized that at some point over the past years I had started to feel tested and resentful. I felt resentful of having to make it work, no matter what, month after month, yet, anxious that if I didn't do it perfectly, I'd lose the merit to conceive that cycle. Clearly, *Hashem* was not agreeing. This isn't about what I would put in and what He would reward me with. Going to *mikvah* isn't about getting rewarded. It's about my connection with *Hashem* and doing what He wants from me. I realized that *mikvah* is MY *mitzvah*, something so precious to Him that He asks it of me again and again.

As I marked my *niddah* status in my calendar I thought, "*Hashem*! That *mikvah*... that *mesiras nefesh*... that was all for You."

When Mindy gave birth to a baby nine months later while I was once again *niddah*, I cried for a third time.

But these tears were not for the *bracha* that I thought I had earned, they were for the *mitzvah*.

A *mitzvah* that would always remain precious to me and precious to *Hashem* for the sake of the *mitzvah* itself.

Story Eleven
A Little Nudge

I was away from home when the call came asking to schedule an appointment to use the *mikvah* the next evening. I frequently get calls from travelers inquiring about the *mikvah* in the resort town where we run a *Chabad* House, and the calls and conversations are usually very to the point. They usually consist of arranging a time, sharing the location of the *mikvah*, and "okay, see you later!" This call though, took longer than usual as we went back and forth trying to find a time to meet at the *mikvah*.

"I'm here with my entire family, " she told me more than once as we went in circles trying to work out a suitable time for both of us. The conversation meandered a few times, and at one point it became clear that while she was looking to schedule an appointment for the next evening, she was really able to *toivel* that night.

I often ponder on whether or not to speak up in this kind of situation. Sometimes I feel like if it's been brought to my attention, I should say something, and sometimes the feeling is that it's not my place and it's not my business. I'm really not sure what makes me lean towards a certain way other than *hashgacha pratis*.

That day, I had a feeling that I should say something. "If you can go tonight," I asked, "why wait until tomorrow?"

"Oh, but it's so soon and it's really complicated to get away... I'm here with my whole family and how will I explain...?"

Since the only reason she was delaying her *mikvah* night was inconvenience, I decided to do my best to make it more convenient for her as I continued to encourage her to try to make it that night. It really was a challenge to find a suitable time, and in the end, we set an appointment for midnight.

While I was glad to be able to help her go to the *mikvah* on time, later on, as I locked up the *mikvah* in the wee hours of the morning, I had an uncomfortable feeling that I had stuck my nose where it didn't belong. The feeling of having overstepped my boundaries was intense.

After that night, I put the whole story out of mind as our lives continued as usual. About a year had passed when my phone lit up with this woman's number. I didn't remember who she was, but as she recounted the story, the episode resurfaced in my mind.

"Hello?"

"Hi, this is –. We met last year around this time when I used your *mikvah*? I had my whole family here on vacation and you convinced me to go on time and not push it off?"

"Oh yes, sure, I remember. How are you?"

"Well, I've been meaning to call you for a while… Last year when I called, you convinced me to go to the *mikvah* on time, even though it would have been way more convenient to delay it. At that point, I hadn't been able to conceive for ten years and had all but given up hope, but after that *mikvah* night I became pregnant! My baby is almost three months old and I wanted to call to say thank you. If you hadn't pushed me that day, she wouldn't be here. You're really the one who made it happen!"

After wishing her *mazal tov* and much "*Yiddishe nachas*", I hung up the phone, speechless and so thankful to *Hashem* for giving me the opportunity to be a part of bringing a precious *Yiddishe neshamah*, a Jewish soul, into the world.

Story Twelve
His Mother's Lasting Impact

My mother-in-law was married in the former Soviet Union many years before immigrating to the United States. She would often tell us about how the government forbade the building, upkeep, and use of *mikvahs*; and the *mesiras nefesh* and self-sacrifice women had for the mitzvah of *mikvah*.

One of her favorite stories was about her sister-in-law, who was a very small, slight woman. She wasn't of very robust health and was often sickly.

One evening she approached my mother-in-law to ask if she would accompany her to the *mikvah*. At that time, there was no *mikvah* in the city, and women would *toivel* in the Black Sea. The Black Sea is not a soft, gentle ocean-front beach with little rippling waves. The coast there is very rocky and dangerous, and the sea itself can be very rough. On that particular winter night, *toiveling* in the Black Sea meant dipping into freezing, raging, inky black water.

My mother-in-law tried to dissuade her sister-in-law from going.

"It's so very cold, and you are ill and not strong. You don't need to put your life in danger in this way!"

But her sister-in-law wouldn't hear of it.

"This is such an important *mitzvah*!" She countered. "How can I let the cold get in the way?"

In the end, as my mother-in-law would tell us, the argument was won by her sister-in-law, and they went together to the Black Sea.

My mother-in-law would always point out at this point that she was right! Her sister-in-law did develop pneumonia from that *mikvah* night and was very ill for an extended period of time. But her sister-in-law was even more right, she would say, because she also conceived that night and gave birth to a healthy baby boy.

That little boy grew up to be a giant in Torah. A beloved Rosh Yeshiva, a brilliant genius, who educated thousands and thousands of students with a profound love of *Hashem* and His Torah, with vivid insight and wisdom for sixty-four years.

Sixty-four years of spreading Torah across the world all born from that night of true self-sacrifice in the freezing, raging waters of the Black Sea.

Story Thirteen
Overcoming my Water Phobia

My story begins when I was in seventh grade with a camp trip to a water park. My friends and I were having a wonderful time going from one ride to the next, when I suddenly got caught underwater. I clearly remember being stuck there, submerged for quite some time. The feeling of being flooded and unable to breathe was overwhelming, and the fear that I wouldn't be able to get out was paralyzing. Thankfully, I was rescued from the water, but even though I was physically fine after the incident, the emotional trauma left me with a heightened fear of water.

Because of the trauma, I don't even remember the exact details of how I became stuck, but after that day I wouldn't go close to a pool, let alone step foot into one. Over the years my water fear worsened until it became a full-blown water phobia.

I got engaged to my wonderful husband almost exactly ten years after my near- drowning incident, and shortly afterwards the time for *mikvah* arrived. My water fear didn't present in a huge way up until that point. I avoided water when I came across it, but on a daily basis I didn't think much about it. But now I had to face the fear in a much more present and constant way. I suffered from extreme anxiety for the whole week leading up to the day of my immersion. What should have been a wholly spiritual experience of renewal and beauty, was full of fear and panic.

When the time finally came for me to *toivel*, I could hardly breathe. I had an extremely unpleasant, fearful experience, and I was completely overwhelmed. The thought of having to do this every month made me so scared and confused.

Thankfully I became pregnant very soon after my wedding, gave birth nine months later, nursed clean for fourteen months, and then got pregnant again, so going to the *mikvah* wasn't part of a monthly routine. In my first four years of marriage, I can count on one hand how many times I had to go to the *mikvah*, and each time was traumatic. After those four years of pregnancy and nursing, I began to have a regular monthly cycle and *mikvah* started becoming a monthly ritual. It was an awful experience each time. It wasn't just the few minutes of going underwater; the whole day was so hard for me. I was a total wreck from the morning, and sometimes even days, before.

I hated every second of *mikvah* and everything related to it. My fear and anxiety started to distort my thinking and I found myself filled with so many questions about why *mikvah* is even something a woman needs to do. I realized that the questions were coming from my fear, and I finally reached a point where I realized I had to make a choice. Either I could continue this way, struggling each month and hating it, or I could choose to make changes and start *living*. I am grateful that I chose thriving over surviving.

The first step on the journey was investing in lessons on how to overcome my fear and be able to enter the water calmly. It took a lot of strength and courage, but I kept pushing. I spent a lot of time and money, but I knew it would be worthwhile.

I am so happy I took that step and took those lessons. After time and practice, water wasn't my worst enemy anymore. I was able to start realizing that the fear had taken away so much serenity from my life.

After achieving the goal of overcoming my water phobia I was ready to move on to the next step, which was to make *mikvah* a reparative experience for myself. With the help of my therapist, I tried many different *mikvahs* until I finally ended up in the most incredible place. I now travel over an hour when I need to go to the *mikvah*, but it's completely worth it.

From the first moment I opened the door to 'my' *mikvah*, I felt nurtured, pampered, and understood. I was given as much time as I needed, and the constant reassurance helped me through. Each time

I went to the *mikvah* in this positive and supportive environment, my fear lessened and the experience became better and better.

Once my fear of water subsided, I was able to start thinking clearly. I realized how beautiful this time can actually be, and I was able to devote my time and energy to making *mikvah* a positive experience. I immerse in the *mikvah* monthly with the pure intention of connecting to myself, *Hashem*, and this beautiful *mitzvah*. Today I am grateful for how far I have come. I even found myself saying last month that I'm actually looking forward to going to the *mikvah*, something I never could have imagined for myself a few years ago!

My relationship with the water becomes purer each time I go. Less fear makes way for more healing, excitement, and renewal; and the *mikvah* has become a place I feel safe. *Hashem* gave us women this precious *mitzvah*. It's a time to connect with Him and a time to connect with ourselves. How lucky we are to have this special time alone with *Hashem*!

If you are out there struggling, there's hope! You too can make *mikvah* a beautiful experience for yourself!

Story Fourteen
Do Something Extra

My teeth chattered as I unlocked the *mikvah* door, hoping that the appointment would be a quick one. Besides being freezing cold outside, it was also *Yud-Tes Kislev* (a huge day of celebration in *Chabad*) and I had been hosting a *farbrengen*, a Chassidic gathering, in my home.

I almost never host evening events because I'm the only one with the key to our remote community's *mikvah*. While I do ask women to please schedule appointments twenty-four hours in advance, you'd be amazed at how frequently last-minute calls come in.

When my son came down with the flu and asked me in the eleventh hour to take over the *farbrengen*, I agreed very reluctantly, and now I found myself in just the sort of situation I had worried about.

The phone started to ring just a few minutes after the *farbrengen* began. At first, I wasn't going to answer it, but when the caller tried a second time and then a third, I realized it must be *mikvah* related. I tried to convince the caller to try another *mikvah* as she was located at about the midpoint between ours and the other option, but she was adamant that she wanted to come to ours. I warned her that the *mikvah* would be cold.

We live in a very warm location and our *mikvah* isn't regularly heated. For some reason, that night was unusually freezing cold. She remained adamant. "I need to use the *mikvah*. I don't care if it's far or cold, I'm coming!"

I arranged to meet her at 10:00 p.m., and when the time came, I apologized to my *farbrengen* guests, and rushed across the street to unlock the door.

The woman was waiting for me, and as I showed her in, she asked me if she could share why she was so insistent on using our *mikvah*.

"I was here last winter," she said. "I came back to say thank you."

"My husband and I had been trying to conceive for eight months and I was feeling very down. We got to talking and you encouraged me to take on an extra *mitzvah*. 'When you want something extra from G-d,' you said, 'try to do something extra for Him.'"

"I had grown up in a *frum*, religious family, but as I got older and married, I became more lax in my observance. So after your encouraging words, I took upon myself to be careful about covering my hair."

"I started as soon as I left the *mikvah*, and I became pregnant that month! Our baby is beautiful and healthy, thank G-d, and I decided I wanted to come back to your *mikvah* after giving birth to thank you."

On her way out she thanked me again as she reached up to touch her hair covering.

"I never go out without it, " she told me. "I'm so thankful for the *mikvah*, the *mitzvah*, and my beautiful baby."

Story Fifteen
Segulot v'Matanot!

I should have realized when the call came in that this was not going to be the typical *mikvah* appointment. A *Shlucha* from a few hours away was on the line.

"Someone from my community is going to be near you for *Shabbos* and she needs to use the *mikvah* after *Shabbos* ends, " she began.

Typical enough, I think. Most women call for themselves, but every once in a while, you'll have a *Shlucha* or *Rebbetzin* call for someone who's new to the *mitzvah*.

"She's a *kallah*," the *Shlucha* continues, "We know the family and all her preparations have been done properly. You can take her to the *mikvah*."

"Okay, I'll expect her call," I answer.

"You should probably call her."

"Um, okay." This is a first. I've never called someone to make an appointment *for them* to come to *mikvah* before. It's always been the other way around.

I take down the number and hang up, unsure of how to proceed. Then I dial. Just do it, right?

Voicemail.

I try again a few minutes later and an enthusiastic young woman answers the phone. "Oh hi! Yeah, I'm going to be in your area with my mom, and I'm getting married, and yeah, if I could come to your *mikvah* that would be great!"

We arrange to meet at 8:00 p.m. on Saturday evening and I'm

about to hang up when she nonchalantly asks, "Hey, can my mom come too?"

I don't give it much thought as I answer, "Sure. Anyone you want can come with you."

As soon as I turned on my phone after *Shabbos* there's a message from the *kallah*. "Gonna be a little late. Is 8:30 okay?"

I message back a quick, "Sure," and head to the *mikvah* to get things ready.

At 8:25 my phone buzzes again, "So sorry. 8:45?" I grit my teeth and send back another, "Sure."

It's going to be a long night. Sunday is my busiest day of the week and I typically get up around 5:00 A.M. If this appointment gets any later, I'm going to be exhausted tomorrow.

But *mikvah*. I'm in it for the long haul.

The Very. Long. Haul.

After a few more texts, each pushing her arrival back by just fifteen more minutes, the *kallah* messages me at 9:30. "Be there in five. My mother-in-law says she's there and can't get in?"

Mother-in-law? At the *mikvah*? Another first. Also, I'm at the *mikvah*, and she is definitely not where I am. I check the security cameras and find her waiting at a different entrance to the building, so I buzz her in and go to meet her.

"*Shavua Tov*[9]!" A diminutive woman with a strong Israeli accent flings her arms around me as I open the door. "We are having a *simchah*[10]!" She gestures widely with her hands, smiling and bobbing her head. "I just have a bag to bring, you can to wait?"

'A bag' turns out to be five bulging canvas shopping bags, shlepped inside by a beaming mother-in-law with no *kallah* in sight. When I explain that the *mikvah* is in fact on the other side of the building, I am recruited to help carry two of the bags over. One is quite heavy, the other lighter but boxy, bulky, and awkward.

"So what's in the bags?" I ask conversationally as the wiry Israeli mother-in-law leads me down the hallway (which feels rather backwards, since I knew where we were going and she had no idea, but I'm just going with the flow at this point).

9   the customary greeting after *Shabbos* which wishes one a good week.
10   Hebrew for celebration

"*Segulot! Matanot!*[11] For a *kallah* the *tevilah* is special!" She beams exuberantly. I have taken many *kallah*s to the *mikvah*, and it truly is special, but it is always sans the protective charms and gifts. Also, sans the mother-in-law.

In the waiting room, the mother-in-law busies herself emptying her bags. Plates of fruit covered every inch of the table, and boxes piled up on the couch. "What is all of this?" I ask. I am treated to an explanation of every item in a mix of Hebrew and accented English. *Sefardim*, she tells me, have a special ceremony at the *mikvah* before the wedding. Fruits from all the *sheva minim*[12], blessings, and gifts. "For *haKallah*!" She finishes, beaming.

I nod as I take in the scene. Never in all of my years as a *mikvah* attendant have I seen anything even remotely like this. My community is heavily Ashkenazi and I have never even heard of, let alone had the opportunity, to experience this custom. To say I am feeling lost would definitely be an understatement. And 'haKallah' still hasn't arrived.

My phone buzzes before I can think of what to think. "Here, " reads the message, as the doorbell rings. I open it to a heavily made-up middle-aged woman dressed to the nines, with designer sunglasses perched on her head and a designer accessory in every accessorizible location. With her is a sweet looking young woman who appears slightly overwhelmed.

Kallah and her mother have arrived.

Mother eyes mother-in-law with suspicion as she enters the waiting room with her daughter, but mother-in-law is unperturbed. "*Chamudee*[13]!" she shrieks; and runs over to hug the *kallah* and kiss both cheeks. Mother expertly sidesteps as mother-in-law moves in to hug her, leaning in for a quick air kiss instead, missing widely as she attempts to reach mother-in-law's diminutive height from her perch on three-inch heels.

"Let me show you the preparation room." I gesture for the *kallah* to follow me. Mother and mother-in-law get in line, and I walk the entourage through the room, pointing. "Here are the drawers with supplies, checklist, towels, and robe. Press this button for the jets in

---

11 Hebrew for rituals and gifts
12 The seven special fruits of the Land of Israel listed in the Torah
13 A term of endearment in Hebrew for "cutie"

the shower. You can text me when you're ready and I'll open the door to the room with the *mikvah*"

Kallah looks uncertain, Mother looks slightly bothered, *Shvigger* looks absolutely thrilled.

Nobody moves.

"Let's step into the waiting room." I motion towards the door. "And give the young bride the time and space she needs to prepare.

Kallah looks relieved. Mother looks slightly bothered. Shvigger looks devastated.

I corral Mother and *Shvigger* and lead them into the waiting room, where *Shvigger* continues laying out the contents of her many bags and mother perches precariously on the edge of the overflowing couch, watching.

After some more re-arranging, *Shvigger* pipes up. "For *HaKallah* the *tevilah* is so special!"

When she says this, I am inspired to answer,

"Not just for the *Kallah*. For every Jewish woman. You too."

"*Ken*, I know, " she replies looking wistful.

Kallah texts me a while later, and I take her into the room with the *bor*. "It's quite the party," she tells me resignedly, nodding at the door. I smile and ask her if she asked them to come along.

"My mother does everything with me." She pauses. "My mother-in-law is very excited."

You can say that again.

When *Kallah* comes out of the preparation room after her *tevilah*, *Shvigger* is ready. She grabs her hands and starts to dance, singing and ululating "lee-lee-lee-lee-lee!" She grabs Mother as they dance past, and mother dances a few steps, getting into the excitement. Maybe it's the hour?

Shvigger may be small but she's got big plans. We're all led to the table where she encourages us to say "*brachot*" on each of the *shivas haminim*, starting with a bottle of wine. *Kallah* and Mother join her, getting into the excitement.

"Now henna!" *Shvigger* announces, pulling out a cone. Okay, I think I've heard of this one. She draws designs on *Kallah*, Mother, and herself. I politely decline.

It's a quarter to twelve when she announces "*Matanot LaKallah!*"

and begins to stack boxes on the table. As *Kallah* opens the first one *Shvigger* trills again, "lee-lee-lee-lee-lee!". *Kallah* unwraps a box of lingerie and I decide it's time to be done. '*Ad kan*' as *Shvigger* would say.

"Wow, this has been really beautiful." I say, too loudly, just in case *Shvigger* plans to sing again. "It's been wonderful, but I'm going to have to say goodnight. I've got to get home now." *Shvigger* looks devastated, but begins to pack up her bags. *Kallah* and Mother help her, and I herd the excited threesome out the front door just after midnight. As *Kallah* leaves with her mother I wish her "Mazal Tov!" and ask her if she intends to continue to use the *mikvah* once she's married.

"Yes, definitely," she answers me, excited. "It was beautiful, and I really feel it's an important part of my marriage."

I'm blown away. What a special custom and what a special young woman!

She winks as she walks away. "Not with my mother-in-law, though."

Story Sixteen
Just in Time

The closest *mikvah* to where I lived growing up was about twenty minutes away by car. While not terribly inconvenient on a weeknight, it definitely posed a problem on *Shabbos* and *Yom Tov*. My parents dreamed of building a *mikvah*, but finances were tight and various more pressing projects took priority over the years.

Finally, twenty years after they moved in, my parents decided the time had come. A capital campaign to raise the necessary funds was started, and the building of the *mikvah* began.

It took a while, but eventually construction of the beautiful, modern *mikvah* was completed on *Rosh Chodesh Adar*, just two weeks before *Purim* and six weeks before *Pesach*. All that was left to do was to fill the *bor*, the reservoir that contains the rain water, and all we could do was wait (something we had actually gotten quite used to in the *mikvah*- building process).

It was really the perfect time of year, the middle of the winter, and precipitation was not lacking. A big rainstorm on *Purim* filled the *bor* about 75%, and we were sure that the next big downpour would finish it off, so we waited. And waited. And waited.

While there was no lack of rain after that, it seemed like the clouds were deliberately passing us by. The rain would be pouring two miles north and coming down heavily three miles south, yet we would only get a few drops and a sprinkle. We tracked the incoming weather, *davened* for rain, and watched the weather on-line as storm after storm would head straight at us, only to veer off course right as it was about to hit us, leaving us with a teaser of a quarter inch of rain.

The *mikvah* filled ever so slowly, reaching about 95% as *Pesach* began. On the first days of *Yom Tov*, another teaser storm blew past us, sprinkling us with just a few drops.

The water that we are talking about is not the water in the *mikvah* pool. Every *mikvah* pool is connected to a *bor* (usually a cement cistern) which needs to be filled with pure rainwater. The *mikvah* pool is connected to this *bor* and is filled with regular water which is changed and filtered as needed. We were waiting for the rainwater to fill the *bor* before the regular *mikvah* pool could be filled with fresh water.

Right before the final days of *Pesach*, my mother got a call from an out-of-town guest. She had heard that there was a new *mikvah* and wanted to know if she could use it on the eighth night of *Pesach*.

My mother explained the situation.

"The *mikvah* construction is complete, but we're still waiting for rain to finish filling the *bor*." She told the caller.

"Great!" The caller replied. "There's rain in the forecast for tomorrow!"

"Even if it does rain, there's no way to know in advance if it will be enough," my mother cautiously replied,.

My mother put down the phone and informed us of the development. Someone wanted to use the *mikvah* on *Yom Tov*! My mother called the *Rav* who confirmed that the *mikvah* could be used as soon as it was full. We watched the sky all day that day and the next (the seventh day of *Pesach*), *davening* for rain clouds to form.

Unbeknownst to us, on the seventh day of *Pesach* the potential *mikvah* user came to our house to meet with our mother and get an update on the *mikvah*.

"If the rain does fill the *mikvah* today," my mother told her, "there won't be enough time to heat the *mikvah* pool water by tonight. The water will be cold. Would you still want to use the *mikvah*?"

"Yes!" she replied.

"If it rains and the *bor* is filled with rain water, allowing us to fill the pool with fresh water, we won't be able to filter the water because of *Yom Tov*. Do you still want to come?"

"Yes!" She said again.

"And if it rains, and tonight it's still raining, will you still come? Another emphatic, "Yes!"

The matter was settled, and the visitor turned to walk out the door when "Boom!" a huge clap of thunder sounded, the skies opened, and within minutes the ground was flooded.

My siblings and I raced to the *mikvah* and watched as the water gushed through the pipe, filling the *bor* with water. We danced and jumped with excitement! The *mikvah* was full!!

That night, our *mikvah* was used for the first time. When my mother told her how long we had waited for rain, the woman who *toiveled* was overwhelmed.

"I feel so blessed." She told my mother, more than once. "*Hashem* himself filled your *mikvah* just for me! It has infused new life and excitement into my *mitzvah* of *mikvah*."

Story Seventeen
Determined

*W*ow' I thought, looking at my calendar. Another Friday night *tevilah*. This would be the seventh or eighth time this year. I had lost track of how many times exactly, and each one had been its own story. Preparing for *Shabbos* and *mikvah* was super busy, especially in the winter when the day was short. On top of that, while I lived literally across the street from the local *mikvah*, it was under construction, and the nearest one was a long, far walk away. To top it all off, walking back into a house full of guests after *toiveling* wasn't exactly my favorite thing to do.

Everything together just felt overwhelming, and using the *mikvah* was becoming very stressful.

Unfortunately, I cut my foot badly on Thursday night, and I couldn't put on shoes. After a hectic Friday hobbling between cooking and prepping, I lit candles, and trudged to the *mikvah* in slippers. By the time I finally got there, I saw three other women standing in front of the door. They explained that the door to the *mikvah* was locked and the *mikvah* attendant was nowhere to be seen. I made a quick mental calculation. My husband would be coming home soon from *shul* with our guests, and I really didn't want to walk in late; but if the attendant came in the next five minutes or so, I could probably still make it in time.

A few more minutes passed and then a few more, until the women I was waiting with began to talk about leaving and coming back the next evening. One of the women started preparing to leave. Another, who said she had older children waiting at home, started to follow.

"Wait!" I called out after them. "I know where the *mikvah* attendant lives. Let me go see if I can get her."

I had never actually been to her house, but I mailed her checks monthly for a *tzedaka* she collected for, so I knew her address. I didn't know the area very well, but I was pretty sure I could find the house. After convincing them to wait a few more minutes, I set off in my slippers to find the *mikvah* attendant.

The house was where I expected it to be, and I called out as I banged on the door, hoping the *mikvah* attendant was home and would hear me.

After a few moments of knocking, the door opened and the elderly *mikvah* attendant stood there, her *tichel* slightly askew, clearly having just woken up. Seeing me, she began to apologize profusely.

"I'm so sorry!" she cried. "I fell asleep near my *Shabbos* candles! I can't believe I left you all waiting! I'm coming right now!"

We walked quickly back to the *mikvah*, she a few steps ahead of me, almost running, and me *schlepping* a few steps behind in my slippers.

Baruch Hashem, everyone was still waiting when we arrived, and we were all able to *toivel*. Since I had arrived last, I was the last to *toivel*, and by the time I got home it was very, very late. My hurt foot was hurting even more than before, and I was absolutely exhausted.

"Okay Aibershter[14]," I davened as I kicked off my slippers, "I need a break. It's been too many Fridays, and this time was extra hard. It's getting to be too much."

Six weeks later I learned that I was expecting, and after that I had a nice long break from going to the *mikvah*. I didn't go again until many months later, after my twins were born.

---

14 The Yiddish word for "G-d"

Story Eighteen
An Unexpected Benefit

When the *Lubavitcher Rebbe* spoke about the initiative to educate women about going to the *mikvah*, he didn't limit the scope to young brides or women of child-bearing age. He encouraged us to reach out to any **married** woman, even if they were many years past menopause.

Whenever a woman has a menstrual cycle, she enters *niddah*, a form of ritual impurity.

It makes no difference how much time has passed after the last time a woman had a menstrual flow. If she hasn't yet immersed in a *mikvah*, she is still in a state of *niddah* and must immerse in a *mikvah* to become pure. This applies even to women who are post-menopausal and haven't had a menstrual cycle for many years. Until they immerse just once, they are still *niddah*.

A wonderful congregant at our Chabad House, let's call her Nina, was interested in studying the laws of *mikvah* and intimacy within marriage, known as *Taharas Hamishpacha*. She was post-menopausal and at first looked at it as an intellectual exercise. After some time and cajoling, she decided that she wanted to go to the *mikvah*.

Nina suffered from a skin rash that caused her a lot of distress and she was worried about how her skin condition would affect using the *mikvah*, and how the *mikvah* would affect her skin condition. She needn't have worried.

A few days after counting her days and going to the *mikvah*, Nina called me.

"I know you said I can only go once, but is there any way I would be able to go to the *mikvah* again? My rash has gone away! My skin hasn't been so clear in the longest time! What an amazing *mitzvah*!"

Story Nineteen
The Final Immersion

I can still feel a tiny twinge of pain deep inside me as I reach my hand out to turn on the bath water. It's been just about six weeks after my complete hysterectomy[15], and I am still somewhat sore. The pain doesn't really bother me though. It's negligible compared to the emotional turmoil that churns inside my heart. Tonight is the last night that I will ever immerse in the *mikvah* for the *mitzvah* of *Taharas Hamishpacha*.

I gaze at my reflection in the mirror. It is partially hidden by the spreading condensation. Just nine years ago, I stood in this exact spot in the *mikvah*, my body nearly trembling with the excitement of taking on a new *mitzvah* and entering a new stage of life. The excruciatingly ironic way my life has come full circle brings tears to my eyes. I swiftly wipe them away. It's not the time for tears yet – I need to focus on committing every part of these next moments to memory.

The steam rising from the scalding water unfurls into opaque clouds that swirl around the bathroom. I take a deep breath, savoring the pure, thick air, and walk over to the light switch to dim the light. It is only in this womb-like environment that I feel safe enough to finish my preparations.

I undress slowly and deliberately, taking a moment to focus on each part of my body as I expose it. The curves I've worked so hard to love. My bare stomach – a roadmap of sacrifice, each mark a reminder of the difficult choices I've had to make. I gently run my fingers over

---

15 Removal of the uterus and cervix. After a hysterectomy, a woman does not get her period and cannot carry a baby.

the newest scar, a furious red slash that shockingly contrasts with my pale skin. I shiver involuntarily despite the room's warmth, suddenly anxious and overwhelmed.

I lower myself into the water, relishing its balmy embrace, and lean back so that I am lying on the bottom of the tub. I submerge my ears in the water and close my eyes, creating a cocoon of sensory deprivation that immediately relaxes me. I take a deep cleansing breath and allow my mind to wander to the tune of my steadying heartbeats.

I think about the role the *mikvah* has played in my life up until this point. I think of the effects its consistent presence has had on my relationship with my husband, and, more importantly, with myself. I'm reminded of the tingles of anticipation that coursed through my body as I jumped into my husband's arms after my first *mikvah* night, and the sighs of contentment each month as I return to the comfort and safety of his embrace.

As a survivor of trauma, the *mikvah* helped me heal, teaching me that my sensuality was something to be celebrated instead of feared, my body revered instead of hated. Each month as I nourished my body with tender care, I allowed my soul to grow stronger and braver as well.

The *mikvah* has also held space for me, supporting me while my tears mixed with its waters as I mourned the loss of a precious pregnancy. While I waited three more years to conceive, it dared me to hope once again, and after each of my children's births, it celebrated joyfully with me.

A faint, metallic taste sours my mouth as it occurs to me that I will never have this type of relationship with the *mikvah* again. I stand up suddenly, shaking my head to free it from this thought. I will not go there yet. Instead, I numb my aching mind by feeling my senses ignite as I wash my body. The water droplets, light and free, create a path down my skin as they drip, with a tender caress from the soap lather as it foams. I relish the harsh pounding of water from the shower head that rinses me off as its strength jolts me back to my focus.

My stomach churns as my hand shakily turns off the shower. The sudden silence is sticky and heavy on my chest, and I struggle to take a full breath. Inwardly commanding myself to breathe, I begin to count- 1... 2... 3...; slowly inhale; 1... 2... 3...; slowly exhale – until my lungs compassionately fill with air. I step out of the tub and firmly plant my feet on the bathroom tile. Checking my body one last time, I cherish the beauty that glows from beneath my skin; a light which is created from absolute devotion to a *mitzvah*. As I reach for the robe to cover myself, time seems to suddenly slow down, each moment becoming more surreal and harder to comprehend.

The *mikvah* attendant enters the room and recites her checklist with the expertise and dedication of a seasoned professional. As I ask her to check my hands, I can feel her gentle touch nudging me to remain grounded. I follow her to the *mikvah*, the pure smell of clean water keeping me present. She takes my robe and subtly averts her eyes, giving me the space and privacy I need to continue. I walk down the steps, feeling the heat of the water permeate my skin.

Baruch Atah Hashem...al hatevilah. Thank You, *Hashem*, for allowing me to keep this *mitzvah* for as long as I did. Thank You for giving me the opportunity to love You by loving myself.

And as I allow my body to be engulfed by this holy water for the last time, I finally let my tears fall.

Story Twenty
The Right Decision

A very good friend confided in me that she and her husband really wanted to have another child. "We're not getting younger," she said "and we always wanted to have more children. We're trying to conceive." While they weren't religious in the traditional sense, she had come to the *mikvah* for many years and had always been careful about the laws of *Taharas Hamishpacha*.

After a few months of unsuccessfully trying to conceive, she and her husband consulted a reproductive specialist and were told that waiting to be able to go to the *mikvah* was causing them to miss a key conception window. This, the doctor told them, was all that was standing in the way of having another child.

Since we had spoken a lot about their decision to try to conceive and then about the difficulties they were having, it wasn't surprising when my friend called me to share the doctor's latest diagnosis and guidance. We discussed the various things the doctor had tested and explained, and I hung up the phone with a pit in my stomach. Although she hadn't said it outright, I understood that she was going to try to conceive without going to the *mikvah*. I was deeply saddened that they would have a child not born in *Tahara* and the holiness of *mikvah* when they had been careful about this *mitzvah* for so long. While I understood the doctor's guidance, the Torah teaches us that adhering carefully to a *mitzvah* is what brings us life not the opposite. It may have seemed counterintuitive for her to go to *mikvah* when the doctor was saying that she would miss her ovulation, but at the same time, I knew that it was *mikvah* that would be the key for her to conceive and not what the doctor said.

A few months later my friend was expecting, and the pit in my stomach grew into a gaping, gnawing hole. I felt absolutely terrible that I hadn't done more to try to convince her to continue to use the *mikvah*. When I called her to say hello, the conversation was stilted and uncomfortable, and I couldn't bring myself to wish her congratulations or '*b'shaa tova*[16]'. My friend understood what was going on right away, and after a few moments of stiff small talk she interrupted me mid-sentence.

"Leah, I went to the *mikvah* on time. I didn't listen to the doctor. I went anyway."

I will never forget the way I felt, holding the phone and listening to those words. My heart turned over inside of me and I was filled with awe. What an amazing sacrifice for a *mitzvah*, and what an amazing return on her investment.

---

16 Lit. "In a good hour". This is a customary greeting to a woman who is pregnant, wishing her an easy birth, at the right time.

Story Twenty-One
Surrender

My grandmothers broke the ice in order to use the *mikvah*. I go despite having an excoriation disorder. The external challenge might look very different, but the commitment to overcome challenges – both within and without – is the same. This is not a story that will give you all the good feels about the beauty of the *mitzvah* of *Taharas Hamishpacha*. There are plenty of those.

This is about sharing how I am here, though it is trying and difficult, to do a *mitzvah* that has been an arduous challenge.

Let me take a step back. When it comes to one's body, repetitive behaviors and disorders can be tricky. If someone is picking at a scab and making themselves bleed it seems so simple to say "stop." But for someone with a skin-picking addiction, or excoriation disorder, it seems impossible. For whatever reason, *Hashem* wired me in a way that once I start, my brain sends me commands to pick until I cave in to its demand. Picking my skin gives me a release from my anxiety. When the tension builds up my automatic response is to indulge in this self-destructive behavior. If you can't relate, I am truly happy for you.

With lots of outside support, I have learned to manage day-to-day life. I have learned many healthy coping mechanisms, and I abstain from behaviors that can lead to a picking episode – that is, until it comes to *mikvah*. It would seem like *halachah* itself is the biggest obstacle and trigger for my old behaviors. The preparation of checking the body for intervening substances was for many years, and still is, a difficult challenge for me.

I used to cry for hours before, during, and after *mikvah*. I felt so alone and at a loss for how to go about fulfilling this *mitzvah* without hurting myself. I am so grateful that today my experience is far from the disaster that it used to be. Keeping it a secret was a form of torture and only buried me in shame. Being honest with the right people helped me come up with a plan that would support me emotionally and spiritually. I am grateful to have a very patient and understanding *Rov* who has given me guidance on how to prepare in a way that would be the least triggering to me. My friend is a nurse, and when I finally unburdened myself to her she helped me come up with a plan in the most unassuming way possible. I am blessed to say that I have only encountered the kindest *mikvah* ladies and understanding women along the way.

I have come to realize that *halachah* is my biggest protector. *Halacha* empowers me by allowing me to rely on the *halachic* definition of clean when I am assailed by desire to pick my skin. I have also come to realize that my triggers are manageable when I can properly identify them for what they are, false triggers.

The most important part of this journey was my learning how to surrender. Before I prepare for *mikvah* I say a *tefillah*, a prayer from the depth of my heart, "Dear *Hashem*, this *mitzvah* is so incredibly hard for me. You gave me this mental illness, and I am doing the best that I can to serve you. Please help me accept the imperfections of my body and help me to surrender and do Your will."

Even today, fulfilling this *mitzvah* comes with anxiety and internal battles. I continue to ask for help before and after I go to keep me focused on what I should actually be doing and not on what my internal voice is telling me to do.

I also spend time meditating. I think about how the same *Hashem* that commanded me to fulfill His *mitzvah* gave me this challenge. How I would not have this exact life's circumstance if I didn't have the deep inner strength to overcome it. I think about how unlimited my *neshamah's* capacity is, how infinite it really is.

I am conscious of my thoughts, because if not my mind will wander. I have learned the hard way that it is up to me to direct my train of thoughts, so it doesn't take me to the wrong destination or fall off the tracks altogether.

Despite the deep struggle, I go. I go because this is my ice to break and my icy water to tread. I go because I am a soldier in *Hashem*'s army. I go, not because it makes sense, but because I am committed to doing *Hashem*'s will no matter how much effort I have to put in. This is my private battle – one that almost no one in my life is privy to – yet the Most Important One, *Hashem*, is "*bochen klayos valev*[17]." *Hashem* looks deep into my heart, sees the absolute challenge and how much I invest in overcoming it, and it gives Him so much joy and pleasure.

And so, while it is not the emotional spa experience I would choose to have, I would not give it up for anything in the world, for it is the most profound spiritual experience. I am transcending myself, overcoming the limitations of my body, and surrendering to *Hashem*'s will for me.

As I submerge in the water, my heart is light, for I know that this is the purpose of Creation. I feel so close to *Hashem*, and nothing, not even an excoriation disorder, will get in the way of my serving Him. And all the icy waters melt in the warmth of my surrender.

(Slightly adapted with permission from EmBRace Magazine)

_____

17   Lit, "checking hearts and minds." This refers to G-d knowing the struggle, thoughts and feelings of each of us.

Story Twenty-Two
His Different Plan

For most of my married life I didn't think much about *mikvah*. It just wasn't a big deal for me. I have 13 kids, *keine ayin hara*[18], and they are all around two years apart. I was always either pregnant or nursing, and I went to the *mikvah* only once or twice in between.

After my tenth child, things didn't quite follow the pattern. I lost a few pregnancies, and then nothing. I was *davening* hard to be able to carry another healthy child to term, but it just wasn't happening.

Around the same time, a student of mine got engaged and invited me to her wedding in Europe. I was excited to go, and even agreed to travel with a woman who had been the *kallah*'s learning partner while she was here in school. She didn't know much about Judaism and really wanted to see an Orthodox Jewish wedding, but she was afraid to travel alone. We planned to fly and spend the weekend together.

The trip itinerary worked out perfectly for my calendar which was usually very predictable. I would be *niddah* while traveling and arrive home a few days before I would go to the *mikvah*. I was thrilled that everything was working out so nicely when suddenly my period arrived early. This was quite the curve ball. The wedding was on Monday and I was scheduled to fly on Thursday and return on Tuesday, but now with my *mikvah* night right after *Shabbos*, I wasn't sure what to do.

I've taught many *kallahs* over the years and I always encourage them to make every effort to go to the *mikvah* on time, no matter how

18 A Yiddish expression for warding off the 'evil eye'

difficult. It is said that from time-to-time *Hashem* sends down extra special *neshamos*, and He chooses mothers who are extra careful with the *mitzvos* of *mikvah* and its timing. How could I continue to teach this with such enthusiasm if I pushed off my *mikvah* night?

I was also torn because of my commitment to the *kallah's* learning partner. She wasn't religious and was looking forward to a weekend of touring and sightseeing, but was afraid to fly alone. How could I let her down now?

I called the airline to see about changing my ticket and was told that there would be a fee of $450(!) per passenger since the itinerary was booked as two one-way tickets. I thought about it and decided not to tell the other woman about the change fee. If she wanted to delay her trip to fly with me, I would cover the cost quietly.

Then I wrote to the *Lubavitcher Rebbe*[19], asking for a *bracha*. The letter I received said, "Now is the time for you to be home with your husband and children." I was blown away, and immediately called the airline to change my ticket to Sunday. Then I contacted my travel partner to let her know that I would be delaying my trip. I gave her the option of joining me on Sunday or to fly alone on Thursday, without any mention of the costs involved. She immediately said she wanted to fly on Thursday sparing me the additional $450 change fee for her ticket.

That weekend, someone called to ask for a service we provide which costs $500, more than covering the $450 change fee. I was grateful to *Hashem* for showing me so quickly that I had made the right decision.

I went to the *mikvah* right after *Shabbos* and flew to the wedding on Sunday. It was a beautiful *simchah*, and I was thrilled to be able to attend. I was even more thrilled a few weeks after I returned home when I discovered I was expecting. The *simchah* was especially beautiful for us nine months later, when our 11th child was born, healthy and well, Thank G-d! *Boruch Hashem!*

---

19 There is a custom that people write letters to the *Lubavitcher Rebbe* (or other righteous individuals) asking for guidance or a blessing.

Story Twenty-Three
Chafifah Preparation at the Airport?

It was one of those hectic, crazy weeks when everything happens at the same time; except in this case, everything was happening at the same time in three different countries, none of which was the one I called home. I would be traveling to a student's wedding in France, followed by a speaking engagement in Brussels the next day, and then on to my daughter's graduation in Israel on the third day.

My student had graciously offered me a round trip ticket to France, and I had booked a flight from there to Israel with a stopover in Belgium. I would fly back to France via Belgium and from there fly back home. The itinerary was a bit daunting and I was *davening* to have the strength to do it all on two feet, when suddenly my period arrived, five days early.

What on Earth was I going to do? This meant that I would potentially have to go to the *mikvah* on the night of my daughter's graduation in Israel. How could I miss her graduation? She had been waiting for months to see me and to miss such a milestone event felt like a terrible thing to do.

Should my husband fly with me? That seemed ridiculously impractical. The trip was only feasible for me with the gifted ticket to France. How would we pay for a full ticket for my husband? And what would we do with all of the kids?

I had no idea what to do.

As I performed my *Hefsek Tahara* five days later, I was still no closer to a solution, but *Hashem* had plans and the *bedikah* wasn't clean.

With my *mikvah* night pushed off to the day after the graduation, I began to rethink my itinerary on the way home, realizing that perhaps I could make it on time if I took a direct flight from Israel to France in the morning and then flew straight from France home that same day.

I called the airline and I was, *Baruch Hashem*, fortunately able to make the switch, albeit for a significant amount of money. It would be a tight connection in France because I would have to claim my luggage and re-check it, but I would be back home on the East Coast in time to make it to the *mikvah* that night.

The wedding was beautiful and the speaking engagement went very well. It was wonderful to see my daughter after so many months and to rejoice in the milestone she had reached and the beautiful, mature young woman she was growing into. We enjoyed our time together that evening, and I woke up at the crack of dawn the next morning to make it to the airport for my flight.

Groggily, I looked up at the flight monitor searching for the correct gate and a flash of red caught my eye. My flight to Charles de Gaulle was delayed.

With my already tight connection now even tighter, I sat on pins and needles at the gate, nervously waiting for the flight attendants to announce boarding. We waited and we waited, until the flight attendant got on the PA to announce a further delay. I quickly calculated and realized that if I wanted to make my flight home, I would have no time to pick up my bags in France. I would have to leave them there and hopefully the airline would forward them to me later.

Accepting this fate, I sat back to wait some more, until finally, after what felt like an eternity, the flight attendant called us to board.

We landed in France 35 minutes before my next flight was scheduled to depart, and I ran like the wind to find my next gate, only to discover that it was in a different terminal! I dashed for the shuttle, where I was met by a formal French security guard who asked politely to see my boarding pass. I frantically whipped out my phone to show him but the battery was dead.

"*S'il vous pla ît, Monsieur!*" I begged. "*Je dois absolument arriver à l'heure pour mon vol!*" (Please, Sir! I absolutely must be on time for my flight!)

Hashem was on my side because at that moment a supervisor

walked up and waved me through to the shuttle. As I rode, I realized what a gift from *Hashem* this really was. Even if my phone had been charged it wouldn't have helped. I hadn't checked in for the flight yet, and had no boarding pass.

I ran through the terminal to the gate, praying the whole way that I should make it before they closed the doors, and arrived to find a packed gate area, and a gate screen displaying the bright red numbers of a delayed flight.

I thought about turning back and claiming my luggage, but then decided not to chance it. I didn't think my heart could handle another mad dash like the one I had just made. I sat down in an empty area to wait for my flight to be called. And waited. And waited. And waited.

The flight was delayed by a few hours, and as I calculated my arrival time, I realized that I wouldn't have time to do my *mikvah* preparation before the *mikvah* closed. Looking around I spotted another gift from *Hashem*. An XpresSpa (or whatever they're called in France) directly across from my gate. The flight wasn't scheduled to board for another hour and twenty minutes, so I walked over and began preparing my nails with a nice mani and pedi, right in the middle of Aéroport de Paris.

My flight was called to board just as I was finishing my pedicure, and I ran to the plane with my heart in my throat. The flight back was uneventful, *Boruch Hashem*, and with no luggage to claim, I made it out of the airport in record time. I walked into the *mikvah* at 9:30, just thirty minutes before closing, and thanked *Hashem* for getting me there on time.

There's no baby at the end of this story. I was in my late forties when it happened and nearing the end of my child bearing years. It might seem that my life would have been made a lot easier if I simply pushed off my *mikvah* by one night. But going to *mikvah* on time is of paramount importance, and every effort we make is infinitely valuable to *Hashem*. Every time a husband and wife are together, special *neshamos*, souls, are created, even if they don't come down into physical bodies, and going to *mikvah* on time is significant, even if there's no chance to conceive.

By the way, they found my suitcase, and dropped it off three days later at my front door. But I would have been thrilled with the outcome of my story either way. I'm so glad I made it back on time.

Story Twenty-Four
Just Do It

Once received a call from a woman in our community who had been Torah observant for many years.

"We're going down to Florida tomorrow for *Pesach*," she shared in a tone that sounded less than thrilled," and you'll never believe how crazy it's going to be."

"We're going to *yehupitz* – the middle of nowhere! And it's my kind of luck that *seder* night is my *mikvah* night! We're supposed to be hosting guests, and I can't imagine hosting without wearing makeup! And the best part is that there's no *mikvah* in walking distance; if I want to go that night, I need to use the ocean..."

Her voice trailed off in a half questioning way.

"Why are you calling me?" I asked, a joking tone in my voice to match the *kvetch* in hers. "Do you think I'm going to give you permission to move your *mikvah* night?"

We bantered for a bit, but my message came across loud and clear, and she hung up having gotten the hint that, make-up and ocean notwithstanding, *mikvah* shouldn't be pushed off.

That winter, nine months after that *Seder* night, she welcomed her beautiful baby girl.

Story Twenty-Five
Mesiras Nefesh American-Style

I always hear stories of *mesiras nefesh*, women's self-sacrifice, to immerse in the *mikvah* in Russia. There were women who would break the ice to immerse in a freezing river or would be separated from their husbands for months at a time while they were hiding or when they would both be on the run without access to a kosher *mikvah*.

But that was 80 years ago in Russia. Today we (mostly) don't break the ice, and our *mikvahs* are beautiful and easily accessible. But I once heard from my *Rebbetzin* that we have our own challenges and opportunities to show how precious the *mitzvah* of *mikvah* is to us.

For example, there was the time I had to go to the *mikvah* on *Seder night*, which also happened to be right after *Shabbos*. It was really crazy. I had invited a few guests, whom I tried to uninvite when I realized it would be my *mikvah* night, but they really really didn't want to be uninvited. No matter what excuse I gave them, they insisted they wanted to come anyway. I remember running out of the house as soon as *Shabbos* was over, mumbling some excuse about forgetting something and needing to meet up with somebody. Nobody could understand what I was talking about. Honestly, even I didn't know what I was talking about.

I ran to the *mikvah* and ran back, and somehow the *Seder* happened, guests and all. And that *Seder* night I conceived my daughter Rivka, whom we named for Rivka Holtzberg who made the ultimate sacrifice for *Yiddishkeit* when the *Chabad* house she ran in Mumbai, India was attacked. Terrorists brutally murdered Rivka, along with her husband, two children, and six of their guests, solely for being Jewish.

My *Seder* night *mikvah* doesn't hold a candle to that kind of *mesiras nefesh*, but my daughter's name, Rivka, reminds me that for most of us it's our little stretches, all strung together over a lifetime, that show *Hashem* how precious His *mitzvos* are to us.

Story Twenty-Six
You Never Know

One of my children was born with a heart defect that required open heart surgery. We stayed in the hospital for five weeks which felt like an eternity. Really, it was a huge miracle because we could have been there for many months, but *Baruch Hashem*, the surgery was successful.

One Friday morning, five weeks after she was born, we were given the all clear to take our princess home for *Shabbos*, on the condition that we came back on Monday morning for a final evaluation.

"If things look good on Monday," the lead pediatrician on her team told us, "we can discharge you guys for good!"

We were thrilled to tell our parents that the baby would be coming home on Monday night, and they quickly made travel plans to be at our house when she arrived. It was amazing, but also crazy, because Monday night was my *mikvah* night!

I'm sure you can imagine how I felt and the looks I got when I mentioned casually that I was going out. I can only imagine what people said (and thought) while I was out of the house, having left my medically fragile newborn behind.

While it was far from a convenient time, the holiness and importance of *mikvah* were essential to me. It would have been so easy and understandable if I didn't want to leave my newborn, but I knew that this was something I needed to do for myself and my marriage; and if *Hashem* chose this night to be my *mikvah* night, then there was absolutely no way I was going to push it off!

Story Twenty-Seven
Nuu...?[20]

My sister was getting married, and wouldn't you know, the night of the wedding ended up being my *mikvah* night. *Boruch Hashem*, I'm really not the type to wear makeup. Couple that with a small wedding (a super small wedding) and it wasn't going to be such a big deal.

Except that even without the makeup, it was still going to be a big deal.

The *chuppah*[21] was called for late afternoon, before nightfall, which meant I'd have to get myself and all the kids dressed for the wedding, get to the venue and mingle, leave after the *chuppah* to *toivel*, and come back with some sort of plausible excuse for why I had disappeared.

Then I had a *shaila*[22] on a *bedikah*, and I took it to Rabbi Hendel *ob"m* from Montreal. I was really hopeful that the *bedikah* would be no good so I wouldn't have to go to the *mikvah* on the night of the wedding, but Rabbi Hendel said it was okay.

"Um... if it's good, that means that my *mikvah* night will be the night of my sister's wedding..." I trailed off, not having the courage to fully finish the thought to the Rov.

"Nuu.....?" was his reply.

Maybe he hadn't understood? I knew English wasn't his first language so I tried again. Slowly and more clearly this time.

---

20 Lit. "And so...?"
21 Marriage ceremony
22 Question

"My sister is getting married in a few days, and if this *bedikah* is good, then I'll have to go to *mikvah* on the night of her wedding."

Rabbi Hendel looked at me for a long moment and then replied again. "Nuu....?"

And I understood.

His "*Nu*" was so full of *Ahavas Hashem* and *Yiras Shomayim*, such pure faith and devotion to *Hashem*, all intermingled and together with the way he looked at me. I understood completely, and it changed my whole attitude towards the situation.

It was so beautiful, and such a powerful lesson for me. Whenever *mikvah* feels like a struggle or a stress I try to tap into that "Nuu....?" full of love and awe and the beauty of sacrificing for a *mitzvah*.

But then came the practical part. I needed to be at the wedding and I needed to be at the *mikvah*. After researching body doubles (joking!), I decided on a plan of action.

After the *chuppah*, I turned to my mother. "Ma, I need to bring the baby home. She needs to sleep in her own bed with a babysitter she's comfortable with," I tried to say as casually as possible, my heart beating in my chest.

"Um, ok?" was her confused response. I'm usually super laid back about my kids' bedtimes and where and when my babies sleep, so this was very out of left field. She was about to walk away when she did a double take. "Wait, wasn't it your idea in the first place to have a babysitter at the hall so the kids can just be here and people don't have to go back and forth?" She was completely bewildered.

Oh yeah. It was. Um...

"I meant the bigger kids, Ma, but not the baby. I don't want the baby to be with some random person she doesn't know in the hotel. She needs to sleep in her own bed with someone she knows."

"Um, ok? Whatever?" Distracted by a relative vying for her attention, my mother didn't press further. I breathed a sigh of relief and my husband and I took off with the baby.

My husband taxied around town, dropping me off at the *mikvah*, picking up the babysitter, dropping her and the baby off at home and then returning to the *mikvah* to pick me up and drive back to the wedding. All this, just so we could have an alibi! My mom looked at me a bit funny when we walked back into the hall after more than an hour, but I just shrugged.

"Traffic." I said, when she asked what took so long.

"Nu...?"

Story Twenty-Eight
An Elevated Mikvah Story

The very first time I went to the *mikvah* after my wedding was a story to remember. I chose a different *mikvah* than the one my mother normally used, so I wasn't familiar with it.

My husband drove me that night and was going to wait for me in the car. We followed the directions (this was before the days of GPS) with no trouble, but when we arrived, we found the entire area surrounded by gates which towered over my six-foot-tall husband. And they were locked! We searched for another entrance, but couldn't find one.

The *mikvah* was located in a *shul* building and the attendant had told me that it was around the back, so we drove around to look for a back gate, but again there was no way in (It was also pre-cell phones, so I had no way to call anyone).

We circled the complex again in the dark, looking for a door or a gate or something. Anything! But we couldn't find any sort of opening other than the locked front gates. We circled a second time, starting to worry that we would have to turn around without a *tevilah* and wondering what we should do next. We were newlyweds and totally inexperienced and I sent up a silent prayer from the passenger seat that I should just be able to *toivel* properly that night without any problems.

As we came around the front for the second time I was beginning to feel a bit desperate. I needed to find a way in. Any way in at all. I scanned the front wall frantically, looking for a way to get over or through, when I noticed that the fence adjoining the property next door had a lower wall.

"I'm going to climb over the wall." I told my husband of less than a month. "Don't look!"

I honestly don't know what I was thinking. The side wall was lower but it definitely wasn't *low*, and I was definitely not the wall climbing type, but I picked up my skirt and climbed over that wall, praying that nobody was watching.

Finally inside, I found the complex completely deserted. I tried the door, but it was locked, and I began to think about trying the windows. Then I remembered that the *mikvah* was at the back of the building! I ran around the back of the *shul* and knocked forcefully, almost wildly on the back door. I had to get in! I just had to! After just a moment the *mikvah* attendant opened the door. Needless to say, she was a bit shocked by the intensity of my banging, considering that I had an appointment and she had been waiting for me right inside. When I told her how I had gotten into the complex, she looked exasperated.

"Oy the men! It's so frustrating! They walk out after *maariv* and lock the gates. They just don't think!"

It took a while for my heart to slow to a normal rate, and I *toiveled* with relative calm and peace of mind, but anytime there's any kind of difficulty to get to *mikvah* and I wonder if it's worth the effort, I think about that very first time, and I know that for *mikvah* I'll climb over any obstacle.

Story Twenty-Nine
Pop!

My *mikvah* night fell on the same night as my nephew's *Bar Mitzvah*, and my husband suggested that I push it off. *Baruch Hashem*, we had five or six little kids, and he felt that it would be too much of a bother.

"You're going to be so stressed," he said. "It's not going to be worth it. Just push it off."

But I was determined to make it work. I knew pushing off *mikvah* was not something to be taken lightly, and I wanted to try my utmost to make it happen on time.

It was winter time, so I was able to plan to go to the *mikvah* before the meal. When my kids got home from school that day, I got them ready for the *Bar Mitzvah* and sat them in front of a video. The babysitter I had hired rang the doorbell and I told them I was just going out for a few minutes. I don't think they even heard me to be honest. A video on a school night was a huge treat.

I got to the *mikvah* and jumped in the shower, but when I turned on the water, it was cold. I remembered learning with my *kallah* teacher not to wash hair with cold water before *mikvah* because it can cause tangles, and I was so disappointed. I had done everything I could think of to make it to the *mikvah* on time, and now the water was cold.

Then I stopped myself.

"It's just the *Yetzer Hara*[23]," I remember thinking. "It's just the *satan*

---

23 Lit, the evil inclination. The voice inside of us encouraging us to do the wrong thing

trying to make trouble while I'm trying so hard to do the right thing."

And as I had that thought, the hot water came on!

"Amazing!" I thought. "You push away the *klipah*[24] and it gets popped like a balloon!"

Baruch Hashem, everything worked like clockwork after that and I was able to *toivel* with no issue and get back in time to make it to the *Bar Mitzvah*.

Hashem helps those who help themselves. All it takes is a little *tracht gut, vet zayn gut* – think good and it will be good.

---

24 Negative energy

Story Thirty
Why Mikvah?

I was just a few weeks shy of my thirty-second birthday and about to get married for the first time. I was very happy and excited, not nervous at all, as both my husband Wayne and I strongly believed we each had found our *bashert* and soulmate. Although I'm not very observant, I am very close with Miryam, the *Rebbetzin* of our *shul*, and she offered to teach me about the *mikvah* and laws of Family Purity before I was married. I agreed to let her teach me, but I had reservations. I was unsure if I really wanted to go to the *mikvah*; it was a ritual that seemed unfamiliar and foreign. I didn't feel like I could tell her, though. I didn't want to hurt her feelings or insult her way of life, so I dutifully came to her house several times to learn.

Most of the *mikvah* rules seemed unnatural and too strict to me. After all, I hadn't grown up with them; it was all new to me. Miryam explained how to check for certain signs during the monthly cycle which meant a woman was a "*niddah*" and couldn't have any type of intimacy with her husband, not even holding hands or a hug, for at least twelve days. I couldn't understand or relate. I even challenged Miryam, and strongly.

"Why can only a woman be in this state? Why wouldn't a man ever be *niddah*?"

It didn't seem equal or fair. Were women second-class citizens? And no intimacy for at least twelve days?

Miryam began to explain to me why women are in the *niddah* state during and following their monthly cycles. I knew the explanation I was about to hear would either allow me to have positive feelings towards the *mikvah* or lead me to view the laws of Family Purity and *mikvah* as an old-fashioned ritual. It was a crossroads, and I listened carefully.

"A woman's body is fashioned to create life." Miryam began.

"This potential for life to grow inside us, puts us on a very high spiritual level, a very pure state. Each month when our period starts and the uterus sheds its lining is not a death, but is akin to a death. The potential for life existed within us and was lost. Therefore, a woman is in an 'impure' state (*niddah*) until this monthly cycle is over (plus seven more days), and she is able to reach her naturally pure, highly spiritual state once again after immersing in a *mikvah*."

"This impure state is not physical; a woman is not considered dirty or physically unclean. It is a spiritual state, similar to when a Jewish person leaves a cemetery, one must ceremoniously wash their hands because being near death puts a person (male or female) into a spiritually impure state. So, a woman who has had her monthly cycle, has experienced within her a kind of "death" (the loss of the potential for life), and must reach a spiritually pure status again. This takes a minimum of twelve days (depending on the length of one's cycle) and requires immersion in the *mikvah*.

"You want to know why a man never experiences this specific state of impurity, although they can experience other states of impurity that would require immersion in a *mikvah*? Are women beneath men, second class? Are women considered dirty? Do men want to 'control' women? I've heard all of these questions before." Miryam smiled. "But isn't the answer obvious? Men don't have that incredible, holy potential for life inside of them.

"They can't do what women can do – grow and nurture life within their own bodies. A man cannot physically reach the very high spiritual state that a woman can reach by growing life inside of himself, and a man also cannot experience what is like a death in his own body, and therefore, cannot experience the spiritually impure state a woman can experience. A man cannot achieve, physically or spiritually, that which a woman can – the creation of life (with the help of *Hashem*)."

As Miryam was explaining all of this to me, it made sense, but it still seemed very 'old-world,' and the practical elements of *Taharat*

Hamishpacha seemed like a major inconvenience. It felt unnatural for a husband and wife not to have any type of physical contact for at least 12 days. I didn't feel that I could ever do it or want to do it. I wondered how keeping physically separate could help a marriage.

"But won't a husband and wife grow apart? Maybe the couple will lose interest in each other?" I asked Miryam.

"In marriage," Miryam explained, "things can get old quickly. That initial 'honeymoon' type of excitement doesn't last. The separation of *niddah*, which usually lasts about two weeks, brings back that feeling of excitement, just like a honeymoon. That old saying, 'Absence makes the heart grow fonder,' is very true: A married couple forced to separate for a period of time misses each other. Instead of losing interest in each other, they are more interested in each other, and the separation brings back those feelings of courtship and honeymoon. Everything seems new again when the couple reunites."

Miryam also mentioned that during the *niddah* period, the husband and wife are forced to talk to each other; they must verbally communicate their feelings. A couple can't look at each other or treat each other as physical objects; they must view each other as friends, confidants, and partners. They must express themselves in other ways besides the physical. This is extremely important in a marriage, where the physical aspect of a relationship may at times overshadow the spiritual or emotional aspects.

Everything Miryam told me made sense, but I was still a bit uncomfortable about actually separating from my husband for two weeks and immersing myself in the *mikvah*. Going to the *mikvah* still seemed empty and meaningless to me; I believed it would feel like dipping into a pool and then just getting out. I felt kind of guilty for my feelings, but I had to be honest with myself and with Miryam. I agreed to try it before my husband and I were married because I saw how important the laws of Family Purity were in Judaism, and didn't want to just ignore or discard such an important tradition, which Jewish women have been observing for thousands of years, but I wasn't committing for the long term. I did tell Miryam that the *mikvah* and its associated laws that I was about to observe for the first time didn't feel right to me; they still felt unnatural and uncomfortable. Miryam was very understanding, and explained that since I hadn't grown up with the concept of *mikvah*, and had little prior knowledge of it, my feelings were very normal. I was glad she understood.

I must admit, the period of separation from my (then future) husband was difficult for me. We weren't religious and I was used to holding hands, hugging, etc. before marriage. I knew that the separation would be over soon enough, and then we would be married. We did use that time to communicate, take walks, and make plans. It was nice, but there was definitely an awkward element.

My to-be-husband went with our Rabbi to the men's *mikvah* for the traditional dip before our wedding, and really enjoyed the experience. As for me, well, that first time in the *mikvah* felt kind of strange; it didn't feel necessary. I didn't feel any different coming out than I did going in, or that I was getting any kind of benefit from it. I didn't feel like there had been any kind of 'death' inside me that I needed to be purified from. I was just me, before and after. But all these feelings changed very soon.

Wayne and I were both very excited about the prospect of starting a family together once we were married. We began to try to conceive right away but a few months went by with no success. I remember feeling very sad and frustrated. I had been going to the *mikvah* with Miryam during those three or four months, and on the way there, I'd tell her my feelings. She offered me hope and was very positive about my situation. This time alone with Miryam was very helpful to me. I think going to the *mikvah* (which you must do with another woman in attendance to make certain you have prepared properly and are fully immersed) encourages women to form relationships, communicate, and help each other. It was just what I needed.

Miryam always told me to pray for something whenever I went to the *mikvah*, right after I immersed myself. It's a powerful time for prayer, but I wasn't sure what to pray for. She encouraged me to pray for myself, for someone else, for anything really. I usually prayed for others, but this time I prayed for myself, for a baby in our future. It was at this point that I began to understand why a woman's monthly cycle was like a death. When a woman wants to conceive, every month that goes by, every menstrual cycle, can feel like a death, a potential for life that is forever gone. I felt it. I really felt it.

After what seemed like an eternity (but was only about four

months), I found out I was expecting. Wayne and I were thrilled. We told our families, and even began to think about names. Was it going to be a boy? A girl? I remember it was Purim when we had just found out, and I dressed as a clown for our Purim party. I have pictures of myself on that day, I looked so happy! It all seemed miraculous and magical to me – a baby growing inside me.

At eight weeks, Wayne and I went for a routine visit to the OBGYN. I couldn't wait! I remember seeing a tiny blip on the screen in that dark exam room, and saying to Wayne, "Look! There's the baby! I see our baby!" I was so excited.

A couple of minutes later we were told, quite abruptly and coldly by a technician, "There's a problem."

"A problem?" I asked, as tears started to form in my eyes.

"There's no heartbeat." The technician answered.

My heart sank. The technician told me to get dressed and wait for the doctor in another office. I was devastated. I had had a miscarriage. There were no symptoms; it was a complete surprise.

Needless to say, Wayne and I were very very sad. I felt like there was something wrong with me. Why did this happen? This is when everything that Miryam had told me about the *mikvah* began to make total sense. Not only had I had potential for life inside me, but an actual life. And I had lost it. This was not *like* a death; it *was* a death. I felt a strong need to go to the *mikvah*. It wasn't just an 'option' or some strange ancient ritual anymore; it was a necessity. I believe that going to the *mikvah* after this experience was more valuable than any kind of counseling or book, or anything else I could try, to help my mental and spiritual well-being.

I really felt like I needed a fresh start, both physically and spiritually, and the *mikvah*, I believed, was the only way to get that feeling.

Four weeks later, I was ready to go to the *mikvah* again. Miryam drove me and filled me full of hope on the way there. I told her I couldn't wait to step into the *mikvah*. I believed the warm, soothing water would feel very healing. And I was right. As I immersed, step by step, I felt that feeling of death that I had experienced leave my body, replaced by the feeling of potential for new life.

A woman's body is made to create life. A miscarriage, or even a menstrual cycle, can feel like an unnatural state for a woman to be in when she is trying to conceive. During this state of *niddah* a woman is spiritually impure; she has experienced a death, or at least something akin to death. How can a woman, one who is trying to conceive and perhaps is feeling frustrated and sad, just act as if nothing has happened, and continue to have relations with her husband? A woman may need a break, to regroup, to think, to feel hope. The separation that the laws of Family Purity and the *mikvah* immersion require allows for this important physical and mental break (and there are potential benefits for the husband too, who may be feeling emotions similar to his wife).

Women who believe the *mikvah* and laws of Family Purity are degrading to women, making women feel dirty or unequal to men, just don't understand. They don't realize the value of the *mikvah*, the feeling of getting a fresh start, both physically and mentally. They don't know that a woman may need some time to herself, to reflect and relax. The laws of Family Purity and the *mikvah* accomplish this. Maybe a woman needs a break from the normal routines of marriage. She needs days to communicate and express herself to her husband in a non-physical way, and he needs to express himself in this way too. How invaluable and unique the *mikvah* is, along with the laws of Family Purity. Yes these laws can be strict and difficult to follow, they require much effort and self-control, but the results are definitely worth it.

Story Thirty-One
"Of Course!"

This story starts with the Communist Russian government outlawing religious practice. *Mikvahs* were closed and the *boros* filled with earth. The KGB kept tabs on the Jewish community, trying their hardest to stamp out any vestige of *mitzvah* observance.

But the women of my great-aunt's community couldn't be stopped. The purity of their families was in their hands and they weren't going to give up the awesome privilege and responsibility that is *Taharas Hamishpacha* without a fight. A clandestine *mikvah* was built and women risked their lives to *toivel* and allow other women to do so as well.

One night there was a knock on my great-grandfather's door. Some knocks inspired fear, but this was the secret knock of *Chassidim*. My great-grandfather was a leader of the *Chassidic* community in town, and everyone knew that they could turn to him to help find a way to make *mitzvah* observance possible, even under the Communists. The two men at the door were quickly ushered in, and a short conversation took place.

"Reb Berel, the *mikvah*," said the first, an older man with a cap and a sparse, greying beard.

"Nu?" was my great grandfather's reply.

"The repairs will be expensive. We don't have the money to fix it, and also to grease the palms of the necessary officials. We need your help," said the younger man, his bright eyes flitting around the room nervously watching the windows and doors.

"We'll work it out," my great-grandfather said. "Please, wait here a moment."

Walking quickly to the kitchen where my great-aunt, a young teen, was helping her mother, my great-grandfather spoke in a low but unwavering voice.

"Bella, I need to ask you something." His tone was serious and his daughter Bella looked up, surprised. "The *mikvah* needs repairs. Costly repairs. And they are coming to me for the money. But all the money I have left is what we have set aside for your dowry. What do you think we should do?"

Bella didn't miss a beat. "Of course, you will use the money for the *mikvah*. What is even the question?"

"Are you sure?" Her father looked her in the eye. "It's unlikely that there will be any money left over. You won't even have enough for fabric for a new dress, and surely nothing to set up a home. Would you like to think it over?"

But young Bella was adamant. The dowry money should go to the *mikvah*.

And it did. Great-aunt Bella's self-sacrifice as a teenager allowed many more women to immerse in the *mikvah*.

A few years after her marriage, great-aunt Bella moved with her family to Tashkent. The Communists had closed the *mikvah* there as well, but the *mitzvah* of *Taharas Hamishpacha* held a special place in Bella's heart. Although she was a mother of young children and any connection with formal religious observance put her and her entire family in danger, Bella made sure that there was a kosher *mikvah* in the city – in her own home!

Although we were close, I never heard these stories from her. Other family members shared them with me when she wasn't around. This was a testimony to the kind of life she lived, completely dedicated to the *Aibershter* and his *Yidden*.

"How could she put herself in such danger?" I asked.

"What greater protection can there be," came the answer, "than the *zchus* and merit of the *tahara* of a Jewish woman?"

Story Thirty-Two
My Mikvah Experience

I grew up in a Jewish family of various levels of religious observance. My mother was growing more connected to her Jewish roots and my father was not quite ready to follow. As I grew older, I went at my own pace in keeping the *mitzvos*. I consider myself to be spiritual but there is one *mitzvah* that I've incorporated into my life that I find to be especially beautiful.

Before I got married last year, I went to the "*Kallah* Classes" the Rabbi said were required for him to officiate at our wedding where I was introduced to the *mitzvah* of *mikvah*. I decided that I wanted to take on this *mitzvah* for the sanctity of my marriage and for the family I hope to have soon.

There was a problem, though. You see, I'm scared of water. Scared as in petrified. Like, forget submerging my entire body, I'm afraid to put my big toe in the pool. Since experiencing a near-drowning as a young child, I've avoided all things water, to the point that I failed swimming in high school. But I was captivated by the *mitzvah*, and I decided to do whatever it would take to make it work.

I spoke with my *Kallah* teacher about my fear, she made some recommendations, and the women at the *mikvah* were also extremely sensitive to my needs. They made special accommodations for me to help me feel comfortable. For the first few months I would get extremely anxious at the thought of entering the water, almost to the point of having a panic attack right there at the *mikvah*! Having the same *mikvah* attendant whenever I went helped me. She was sensitive to my needs and patient with me.

Each month, as my *mikvah* date approached, I thought about going to the *mikvah* the entire week before. The number of times I would immerse depended on how courageous I felt. As I went down the stairs, I would take my time and some long, deep breaths. When I hear the word "kosher" said out loud, I breathe a huge sigh of relief. I did it! I feel rejuvenated and rekindled, energy that will hopefully help me for the next time.

Fear of water wasn't my only challenge to overcome. I also struggled with the frustration in my relationship during the days leading up to the *mikvah*, but somehow the tension and agitation of not being able to touch each other, makes the night of the *mikvah* so special because we've been anticipating it for almost two weeks. It's really hard, believe me, but it's also really worth it. The renewal and connection the waiting brings to my marriage are irreplaceable. I feel reborn, clean, holy, connected with my ancestry, excited for intimacy, and, most important, with G-d's will, a beautiful family.

Mikvah and *Taharat Hamishpacha* give me hope for spiritual growth in my marriage, and for the children and family I would like to have. I'm investing in my family's future and I wouldn't give it up for the world. As I immerse in the waters, I feel like a fetus in the waters of its mother's womb. As I leave the waters and feel the cool air against my skin, I draw a deep breath of life into my soul and know that I am different. I feel replenished with a new, deeper energy. I feel as though I am born again and holding a new power; the potential to bear my own child.

Observing *Taharat Hamishpacha* also empowers me with a feeling of self-ownership. There are times I can be touched and times I say, "Don't touch me." The "don't touch me" time is my time to reconnect with myself and reflect. It is a time to be one with my body and do some pampering and self-care. I like to think of my time preparing for *mikvah* as a spa for my body and my soul. Creating a soothing atmosphere beforehand and indulging in my favorite products before I leave the *mikvah* help make it so relaxing and enjoyable. I take my time and relish the experience, and I walk out feeling so beautiful, inside and out, like a special gift for my husband to unwrap when I get home.

Like I said at the beginning, I'm not completely observant, but I wouldn't give up this *mitzvah* for anything. I bless you all with the inspiration to perform this beautiful *mitzvah*, and with the spiritual strength it brings to a Jewish marriage and family.

Story Thirty-Three
Taharas Hamishpacha Saves Lives

My daughter married in 5780, right before the outbreak of COVID-19. A few months after her wedding, while she and her brand-new husband found themselves in lock-down, her father-in-law was admitted to the hospital with Corona.

This is her story.

One *Shabbos*, my brand-new husband and I were discussing how difficult it was to be in *niddah* during quarantine and not comfort each other as we would have liked. We were home all day with each other and emotions were running high, especially with my father-in-law in the hospital. We talked about how the *Rabbonim* had offered leniencies for so many different things except *Taharas Hamishpacha*. We were both annoyed and frustrated.

Just a little while later, my brother-in-law came to our window with an update about my father-in-law, and it wasn't good. The hospital was saying they had done everything they could to help him. There was nothing else they could do. It was almost over.

My husband and I immediately sat down to say *Tehillim* for his father. We were *davening* for a miracle.

I finished the *Tehillim* before my husband and began flipping through the *sefer*[25] I was holding. It's funny, usually I use a *siddur* because I prefer it, but I had just grabbed the first *tehillim* I could find, which was in a *chitas* -a compilation of several *sefarim*. In the back there is a daily Torah thought called the *Hayom Yom*. I flipped to

---

25 Jewish holy book

the *Hayom Yom* of the day, 10 *Nissan*, and read it to myself. "*Taharas Hamishpacha* saves lives, it said.

I showed my husband what I had just read and we immediately resolved to be extra careful with this *mitzvah* as a merit for my husband's father.

Later, my husband told me that he had asked *Hashem* for a sign that his father would be ok, and that's when I showed him the *Hayom Yom*.

From that point we were extremely careful with *harchakos* and all of the different *halachos* of *Taharas Hamishpacha*. On the day I went to the *mikvah*, my father-in-law opened his eyes for the first time.

He has continued to get stronger since then, and a few days ago his doctor told us that from a medical perspective, it's a miracle that he is alive. It makes no sense that he survived from the point he was at that *Shabbos*. Hearing this made my husband and me feel like we were so blessed to be a part of *Hashem's* miracles.

It's amazing to see the words of the *Hayom Yom* come true before our eyes. What can I say? *Taharas Hamishpacha* saves lives.

Story Thirty-Four
The Mitzvah that Kept on Giving

y story starts many years ago, during a particularly frigid Montreal winter, when my *mikvah* night fell on a Friday night in January. The weather was forecast at 22 degrees below zero and the *mikvah* was a forty-minute walk away.

"It's too cold," my husband told me. "It's dangerous to walk tonight."

But I wouldn't hear of pushing it off. I insisted I was going anyway, and after candle lighting, I bundled up in many layers. With determination I opened the door to a frigid blast of air and trekked out into the icy wind, determined to go to the *mikvah* on time. I'm not going to lie, it was a very difficult walk, and I came home that night with frostbitten knees, but it was worth it! I became pregnant with my seventh child that night.

One Thursday afternoon, about three months into my pregnancy, I experienced a spontaneous membrane rupture. In plain English that means my water broke at 14 weeks. This was followed by the loss of a significant amount of blood. Panicked, I rushed to call my doctor, who somberly told me it was all over.

"I'm so sorry, but it seems you've lost your baby. You'll need to come in for a D&C on Monday morning. Please call the office to schedule."

That *Shabbos*, as I'm sure you can imagine, was extremely difficult.

Monday came, as Monday always does, and I checked into the labor and delivery unit for my scheduled D&C. At that time the procedure was typically done under general anesthetic, but my doctor wanted to perform an ultrasound before they put me to sleep. I lay on the bed, trying to stay calm as the ultrasound tech moved the transducer around, when she suddenly jumped up and yelled.

"There's a heartbeat!!"

My doctor, incredulous, asked for a second look. Looking intently at the screen, the ultrasound tech pointed out my baby's steady heartbeat, and announced that my baby was surviving in a tiny thimbleful amount of water!

"Oh, *Hashem*!" I thought, "It's the *mikvah* water! Thank you, *Hashem*, for saving my baby!"

I carried the pregnancy to term(!) and our beautiful, healthy daughter was born on *Motzei Yom Kippur*. Rebbetzin Chaya Mushka had passed away that year and although we are not *Chabad*, we feel a special connection to the *Rebbe*. We wanted our daughter to have a sparkle of the *Rebbetzin's* holiness, so we named her Leah Chaya. I wanted to give back to *Hashem* to thank Him for our miraculous little girl, so when Leah Chaya was four years old, I became a *kallah* teacher, to teach *kallahs* about *mikvah*.

When Leah Chaya was seven, our world turned upside-down. My older daughter Miriam, who was 14 at the time, was diagnosed with a rare type of leukemia. The doctors told us that only a bone marrow transplant could save her, and we began the search for a donor. Our entire family was tested, and can you guess who was a perfect match? That's right, Leah Chaya.

We prepared for the transplant both medically and spiritually, with visits to many doctors and also to many *Gedolim* for *brachos*. One *Gadol*, in particular, gave us a beautiful *bracha* and reassured us that the name Chaya, which we had added to Leah's name, would bring added life to Miriam.

We were advised to give Miriam an additional name, and we chose the name Bracha, asking *Hashem* to continue to fill our lives with the many *brachos* we were so thankful for.

The transplant was a success, thank G-d, and, coupled with intensive radiation therapy, Miriam Bracha went into remission. We were elated, and thanked *Hashem* for the gift of her health. We were devastated, when, together with the news that the leukemia had been eradicated, we were told that Miriam Bracha would never be able to have children. Full body radiation had burned her ovaries, and at just

15-years-old she was menopausal.

This was a difficult prognosis to swallow, but we chose to focus on the positive and be thankful for our daughter's miraculous recovery. Miriam Bracha also took the news in stride, and when she married a few years later it was with the knowledge that children would not come naturally. Imagine her and her husband's surprise when they discovered that she was pregnant, with absolutely no medical intervention! Today she has three gorgeous children, with no medical help whatsoever. Each one is just a precious gift from *Hashem*.

L'fum tza'ara, agra: "According to the investment is the reward." When we do a *mitzvah* that is difficult, we see *yeshuos*[26]. We don't always see its effects right away, but in the long-term our future generations will also see miracles. The bigger the effort, the bigger the reward! May *Hashem* send us *Moshiach*, speedily in our days!

---

26 Extraordinary help from *Hashem*

Story Thirty-Five
A Cross-Country Mikvah

When our *mikvah* first opened, we held a large, inaugural celebration. Women from the entire spectrum of religious observance were invited to tour the *mikvah* facilities, and a well-known speaker addressed the crowd. We were hopeful that seeing the beautiful new *mikvah* and hearing an inspirational talk on *Taharas Hamishpacha* would inspire some more women to take on the *mitzvah*. And it did.

A short time later, a member of the nearby Conservative Synagogue approached me to tell me that she had decided she'd like to go to the *mikvah*.

"Listening to your speaker convinced me that this is the right thing for me and my family," she explained. "I'd like to start using the *mikvah*."

"Now is the best time to start!" And I gave her a run-down of the *halachos*, right then and there in my living room, agreeing that we would follow up in depth later.

She began to use the *mikvah* regularly, but she was very nervous that her kids would realize where she was going. She developed a routine where she would come to the *mikvah* and then go to the ice cream store to pick up treats for her kids as an alibi to explain where she had been. Her kids got ice cream every month for years!

Her dedication to the *mitzvah* became evident during one major winter episode, about three and a half years after she began to come to the *mikvah*, when a massive snowstorm dumped 18 inches of snow on the city, and the governor declared a state of emergency lock-down.

And it was her *mikvah* night.

The plows weren't out, and the streets were completely impassable by foot, covered as they were with 18 inches of fresh snow with no signs of the snow letting up.

"I'm not going to let the snow stop me," she told me on the phone. "*Mikvah* is important to me and I'm coming tonight, whatever it takes."

The *mikvah* was located on our property, so getting there wasn't a big deal for me, but she lived close to a mile away, and getting there wasn't going to be simple for her. But she was determined. So she strapped on her skis and glided across the top of the snow. Or at least she meant to, but skiing a mile across suburban streets turned out not to be so simple that night, with powdery snow conditions, heavy snowfall, and poor light. She fell once, and then again, but she pressed on.

When she finally made it to the *mikvah* she was wet and battered, and she realized that the weather was only getting worse.

"There's no way I'll be able to ski back," she said. "Can I borrow your phone?"

In those days before cell phones, she used the *mikvah* phone to call her husband to ask him to come help her. And he agreed. He'd walk the mile, trekking through the storm, to bring her home.

She *toiveled* and waited for him to arrive, the two of us watching out the window as the snow continued to cover everything with its heavy whiteness. When he finally got there, they walked out into the blizzard together, carrying the skis back through the dark, snowy streets.

And I was left alone, and amazed.

She continued to use the *mikvah* religiously through her 50s, and is proud to remind me that all of her children have married Jewish, something very few of her Synagogue friends can boast.

"It's the *mikvah* that kept them close to their Jewish souls."

Story Thirty-Six
Musings from Main Street

Growing up in a small family, with few cousins, I always dreamed of the day when I would have a large, beautiful Jewish family. I would fill the gaps in my own relatives and boost the ranks of the Jewish people. This dream still stays with me, more than 10 years married.

However, after my first child was born I experienced a major mental health crisis. As per my doctors' instruction, having more children was out of the question. I realized *Hashem* presented me with an unexpected yet pressing job for the time-being. I needed to ensure that my mental health was solid and secure.

There were inevitably going to be many trips to the holy waters on Main Street.

At first, looking at the big picture was overwhelming. This would be my new life. *Mikvah* every month for the foreseeable future. No breaks for pregnancy and no guessing how many months I would nurse clean. Just two weeks on and two weeks off, two weeks on and two weeks off. I tried to wrap my head around it.

In the beginning, I just methodically did the motions. I did what I needed to do and that was it.

But as the years progressed, some funny things happened.

I decided to begin to take the open-ended future cycle by cycle. Like the tides of the ocean constantly moving forwards and backwards, *mikvah* sets a guide for life. Some weeks are me-time and a time to solidify communication skills and awareness of the other's emotional needs; Other weeks our feelings are expressed more physically. In truth, every living being has cycles. We breathe in and then out. We have cycles of time. We have *Pesach* in the spring, and *Rosh Hashanah* in the fall. *mikvah* is the cycle of women which spans the month. The *mitzvah* of *mikvah* keeps me aware and connected to time, helping to provide structure to the otherwise open phase ahead of me. Each moment has a unique purpose to fulfill, and I try my best to make every moment count.

Every time I enter the preparation stage, I make it the time for an intimate, honest reflection and connection with *Hashem*. He made me. He loves me just how I am. He and I alone know all of my physical and mental shortcomings. No-one else is coming to see how well I've checked off my list.

Sometimes we think we can change ourselves by changing our bodies; making our eyes seem bigger or our cheekbones appear higher, but in that preparation room, it's just me and Him. I can be honest with Him. And with myself. I began to look in the mirror and see myself for who He sees. Every inch of me is how our Maker wanted His masterpiece to be. Each stretch mark and scar are the brushstrokes of His work of art. I don't need to change myself. My *chafifah* preparation brings my body back to the way He intended it to be.

Each month, little me becomes a warrior princess, a queen privileged to have a rebirth every month. I have the opportunity to emerge from the *mikvah* a different person: focused, centered, and connected.

As a mortal being, I do not know what the future holds. But every time I slide into the special waters, I surrender my body to the waves, and my will and mind to G-d's Will. I let go of how I thought my life would be, and renew my trust in His Wisdom. He is the Master Planner, Nurturer, and Life-Giver, and He knows exactly what is good for me.

As time passes, the renewed awareness of the gifts of *mikvah* brings a calm peace and rhythm into my life. My soul, connected to the hallowed waters and customs of our foremothers, could realign itself and find space to breathe. My mind and body, supported by medication, trusted counsel, and elevated through *mikvah* to a higher purpose, could rebalance itself.

I'm so grateful for this precious gift.

Story Thirty-Seven
A Light in the Darkness

I grew up in Budapest before World War II as one of eight children. My mother was always careful with the *mitzvah* of *Taharas Hamishpacha*, even during the war. The entire community had been herded into a small ghetto by the Nazis *ym"sh*[27], and we lived in squalor and deprivation. The streets were filthy. There was never enough food, illness was rampant, and the Nazis would shoot people at random in the street. We were living in the shadow of death, and still my mother held on strongly to the mitzvah of *mikvah*.

My father was a prominent man in the community, and when we moved to the ghetto, he fixed up the *mikvah* that was closest to us. By *Hashgacha Pratis*[28], the *Belzer Rebbe* was with us in the ghetto. He was escaping Poland at the time and was traveling through Hungary on his way out. He inspected the *mikvah*, declared it kosher, and used it that day. That night was my mother's *mikvah* night, and she *toiveled* in the newly kosher *mikvah* and became pregnant. When her friends found out, they were mortified and pushed her to have an abortion.

"The *Rabbonim* are allowing it," they told her. "How can you put your life in danger like this? You have eight beautiful children already. Who will take care of them?"

But my mother was adamant that she would not give up the baby she was carrying. "What will I say after 120 when they ask me to

---

27 *Yemach Shemom*- May their names be erased. An expression used when mentioning evil people.

28 Used in this context to show how random events that seem to be coincidental are clearly orchestrated by *Hashem*

show them the beautiful child *Hashem* gave me that I threw away? Absolutely not. I am keeping the baby."

Even though we had so little, throughout her pregnancy she was extremely careful never to eat non-kosher food, and she believed with complete belief that *Hashem* was with us and all would be well. And it was.

One day she was approached by a Nazi in the street. Brandishing his gun, he threatened to shoot her, but another guard stepped up at just that moment and held him off. "Not this one." He said roughly, and pushed my mother along.

She went into labor in the ghetto a few days before liberation, and gave birth to a beautiful baby boy. He was very small, and for a while he was sickly, but he grew and got stronger each day, and today he is a great-grandfather of many beautiful Jewish children, all of whom are here because of my mother's belief and perseverance.

My mother passed away at 94, the matriarch of a large Jewish family, and I am confident that the angels glowed with pride when she showed them the beautiful child *Hashem* gave her, that she held on to with steadfast *emunah*[29] and *bitachon*[30].

---

29 Faith in *Hashem*
30 Belief in *Hashem*

Story Thirty-Eight
Cold? What Cold?

I run a *mikvah* in a large Jewish community. Women from all walks of life use our *mikvah*, and we are *Boruch Hashem* very busy, with 25 to 50 appointments on any given day.

A while ago an incident occurred that really showed me the amazing dedication of so many different women to the *mitzvah* of *mikvah*.

One Friday morning I woke up to the news that a squirrel had chewed through some electrical wires a couple of blocks away and caused a massive power surge in the area. The surge caused extensive damage at the *mikvah*, destroying our boilers and our fire alarm system. We quickly sprang into action, calling plumbers and electricians to try fixing everything as quickly as possible, but unfortunately, there wasn't much they could do for us. There were parts that needed to be ordered and due to the Corona lock-down, stores and suppliers weren't open. There was just no way to pull things together until after the weekend.

At first our board members told me to close the *mikvah*.

"It's a big community," they said. "There are other *mikvahs* that can absorb our appointments."

But I didn't feel like it was right to shut down entirely.

"Let me call the women who have appointments and let them know what's going on. They can make the decision on their own if they'd like to go elsewhere," I told the board. "Maybe there will be a few women who prefer our familiar *mikvah* to a heated one for whatever reason. If they want to come here, I want to be open."

I sat down with the list and started calling.

Let me tell you, I was blown away.

Like I said, we can have 25 to 50 appointments a night, and I called every one of them to let them know what was going on and gave them the option to cancel their appointment. I expected most of them to say they'd go elsewhere, with maybe one or two asking to still come to our *mikvah*. What actually happened was entirely different.

Almost every woman I called took the situation in stride and said she wanted to keep her appointment.

"Oh, you know what, it's not a big deal. I can still come tonight."

"This is just another way *Hashem* is testing us. I can pass this test."

"It's not so terrible. Our ancestors in Russia had to break the ice."

"It's fine. I'd rather just come."

I did this again on Sunday night and then again on Monday, and the responses stayed the same. Friday night really wasn't so bad. The boilers had been on in the morning and it takes time for insulated water to cool down, so it was still lukewarm in the evening, but *Motzei Shabbos* and then Sunday and Monday the water was really quite cold. And still, they came.

A few women did choose to go elsewhere, and a couple commented that it was colder than they expected, but for the most part the women just *toiveled* as if everything was normal. It was so inspiring for both myself and the *mikvah* staff. We watched so many women rise to and above the challenge. It really opened our eyes to the incredible dedication women have to the *mitzvah*.

Boruch Hashem, the boilers were fixed on Tuesday and things went back to normal. But it's an elevated normal. Our entire *mikvah* was, and continues to be, uplifted by those four nights of cold water and the incredible strength and commitment they brought out in our community of wondrous women.

Story Thirty-Nine
Not Obsessed

Onychophagia*. That was the name. A quick Google search had given me the label for the set of behaviors that had driven me since I was a little kid. Obsessive-compulsive nail-biting to the point of not being able to stop.

When my *kallah* teacher had taught me about making sure my nails were cut before going to *mikvah*, I had inwardly laughed. That was not ever going to be a problem for me. My nails were always bitten as short as they could be. I was cheerful at not having to think about what was surely a big part of most women's preparations for *mikvah*.

Little did I know, that my constant nail-biting would only make my *mikvah* preparation harder, not easier. Knowing that I had to rid my nails and cuticles of anything that I would want to take off, made preparing for *mikvah* an anxiety-producing time. Every little extra piece of skin and every little piece of nail made me nervous. I spent hours trying to remove anything that was bothering me, but would invariably find something on my final checks that would make me have to start all over again.

After the *mikvah* lady's multiple assurances that nothing was wrong with my nails and listening to different *Taharas Hamishpacha* review classes, I realized that something was off. Nobody else seemed to be spending hours on their nails.

I decided that maybe I just needed to get manicures. This way the manicurist would do all the work for me and I could just show up to the *mikvah* without worrying about them too much. It worked a few times, but then I was still finding myself at the *mikvah*, anxiously checking my nails and frantically removing skin, which would just make me have to remove more skin in a never-ending cycle.

A quick Google search taught me that I was showing symptoms of an OCD disorder called *onychophagia* or compulsive nail biting. While I couldn't diagnose myself, it sounded exactly like me. I could not stop myself from biting my nails. I would even bite them at times when it was embarrassing for me, as much as I wanted to stop. I could not even stand the sight of them to the point that any sign of a nail peeking out of my skin was instantly bitten off.

After further research and talking to my *kallah* teacher and my *mashpia*, it hit me. The thoughts about my nails were just that. Obsessive thoughts. They were not reflective of my real desire. My real desire was just to have clean, regular looking nails.

Well, enough of that, I decided. If the nail biting was an obsessive behavior, that meant that the obsessive thoughts were coming from the *Yetzer Hora*, my negative inclination. It was just a scam to make me nervous about *mikvah*. I realized I needed to separate my thoughts. I needed to not think about the obsessive thoughts that made me want to remove any bit of nail, and keep my *real* thoughts which were about having nice nails without spending hours getting ready for *mikvah*.

A call to my *Rav* confirmed it for me. As long as my nails were trimmed and clean and there was no flapping skin around my nails, I was good. The next few times I went to *mikvah*, it was really hard for me to be calm at nail-prepping time. I really wanted to just remove anything and everything that could possibly be something. But I knew what the *Rav* said and I followed his guidelines, while shutting my mind from all the other thoughts that tried to invade my head, and thinking instead of how excited I was that it was finally my *mikvah* night.

I still bite my nails. But it's such a wonderful feeling to go to *mikvah* and know that for the time that I'm preparing, I can leave my obsessive thoughts at home. Who knows? Maybe I'll be able to do it at other times, too!

*This story is one woman's personal story. It does not contain medical advice. If you have obsessive thoughts about preparations that

are affecting your ability to prepare in a reasonable amount of time, and if those thoughts last more than three months, then please seek professional help.

Story Forty
Still Grateful a Decade Later

Who sends snail mail anymore? Most of what I find in the mailbox is invitations and junk mail, with the odd bill thrown in for good measure. So when I saw a hand-addressed envelope, I was curious to see who it was from. Still standing at the box, I slit it open.

Inside was a short typewritten letter which read as follows:

"Dear *Rebbetzin*,

As I help my husband prepare for his trip to your city with two of our children, I'm reminded of my visit exactly ten years ago and still feel gratitude towards you. Let me tell you why.

We had been married for close to a year and had not yet merited to have children. My *mikvah* night landed the last night before our flight back home from your city. We called up the old *mikvah* to inquire, but the lady in charge told us something we never expected to hear, ' We don't open the *mikvah* on *Motzei Shabbos*.'

Your *mikvah* still had a few weeks to go until its official opening, but when we told you about the problem, you agreed to open the *mikvah* especially for me.

The story doesn't end there. After becoming '*tehora*' in your *mikvah*, I conceived.

So, this summer, if you happen to see a beautiful nine-year-old *Bais Yaakov* girl walking around your city speaking in Hebrew, know that you had the merit to help her *neshamah* come into the world *b'tahara*.

May you have the *zchus* to help many more ladies bring Jewish children into the world in purity *K'rtzon Avinu Shebashamayim*[31]."

I had completely forgotten about the incident, but reading the letter brought back a flood of memory.

About three-and-a-half years after we got married, my husband took a job as the Rabbi of a small *shul* in a growing Jewish community. Most of the older families in the community were traditional, with a considerable number of the younger crowd making a strong movement towards more religious observance. Understandably, there was some tension between the generations. The younger crowd wanted updates and changes to the Jewish infrastructure, while the older crowd insisted there was nothing wrong with the way things had always been done.

A major point of contention was the *mikvah*. Besides for the fact that it was old and out of date, the *mikvah* was only open five nights a week. Women couldn't *toivel* there on Friday night or *Motzei Shabbos*.

We started raising funds right away and soon began the construction process of a brand new, state of the art, open 363 days a year[32] *mikvah*. We were waiting for the boiler system to be completed so we could run hot water straight into the *mikvah*, not something to take for granted! I'll explain.

One Friday afternoon, about a week before the boilers were scheduled to begin running, the phone rang.

"I'm here from *Eretz Yisrael* with my husband," the caller told me tentatively. "My *mikvah* night is this *Motzei Shabbos*, and I called up the *mikvah* to make an appointment, but they said they won't be open that night. Do you know of another *mikvah* I can use...?" I thought for a moment. There was no nearby *mikvah* to direct her to, but I was loath to tell her that she would have to push off her *mikvah* night when we technically had a kosher *mikvah*. The *mikvah* was already full of water and had been pronounced *kosher* by the *Rav*, but without a boiler system the *mikvah* would be cold. Should I invite her to use our *mikvah* under the circumstances? I figured I'd warn her and let her make her own decision.

"You're welcome to *toivel* in our new *mikvah*," I said. "It's not really

---

31 Lit. "According to the will of our Father in Heaven."
32 There's no *tevilah* on *Yom Kippur* and *Tisha B'Av*.

open yet. It's still unfinished. We don't have a working boiler yet and I won't be able to heat up the *mikvah*. The water will be cold."

"That's fine," she told me. "I don't want to push off *mikvah*. I can *toivel* in cold water. Thank you so much!"

On *Motzei Shabbos* I went to open the *mikvah* and check to make sure things were neat and pleasant. I tidied up the area as best I could and dipped my hand into the *mikvah* to check the water. It was very very cold. Like freezing! I couldn't imagine someone having to *toivel* in such cold water. This was America in the 21st century, not the middle of Communist Russia in 1950, and I felt very uncomfortable bringing someone to *toivel* in such frigid water.

I walked back to the *shul's* kitchen and got to work. I *shlepped* out my biggest pots, filled them with water and set them on the stove. While they were heating up, I recruited two *bochurim*[33] to help me and we emptied a good portion of the water from the *mikvah*. Then we *shlepped* over the big pots and poured the boiling water into the half-full *mikvah*. Then I went back to the kitchen to do it again and again until the *mikvah* was full.

By the time she arrived to *toivel*, the water was closer to lukewarm than hot, but definitely more tolerable than the freezing water I had first encountered.

The young woman came, *toiveled*, and left; and the incident went out of my mind.

As I stood at the mailbox recalling the incident, I was amazed and so thankful that she had taken the time to write a letter and mail it. I was also amazed and thankful for my good fortune, to get to see the other side of the story and the beautiful *brachos* that had come from those big pots of water, boiled and *shlepped* and boiled again, for one woman's one *mikvah* night.

---

33 Yeshiva students

Story Forty-One
Blizzard!

This story takes place when a huge blizzard dumped two feet of snow on our city overnight and the governor declared a state of emergency. The streets were impassable, and even if you could get out, literally everything was closed. Everything except the *mikvah*.

A woman in the community had made an appointment, but she called me earlier in the day, as the snowfall was starting to get heavy, to let me know that she was nervous about coming. She didn't consider herself to be very religious but took *Taharas HaMishpacha* seriously.

"Hey, it's Terry," she said, disappointment in her voice. "It's too bad that I won't be able to go to *mikvah* tonight after all. There's way too much snow on the ground, and it's still snowing."

"I understand your concern," I answered, glancing out the window at the huge drifts of snow that covered the streets. There were cars buried under drifts taller than my toddlers. "I'm from Minnesota! I'm used to driving in snowy weather and blizzards so it won't be a problem at all! I'm happy to come pick you up and drive you to the *mikvah*!"

Now you have to understand, it's not like I had a big SUV or even a small car with four-wheel drive. At the time I drove a plain old minivan with front- wheel drive only. It was definitely not any more suited for the weather than anything she was driving. But I had a chance of getting her to the *mikvah* on time, so I offered.

At first, she was hesitant,

"Are you sure?" she said doubtfully, "there's a lot of snow outside."

But I assured her that I was sure, and, to my delight, she accepted! "Ok, let's go."

It took close to forty-five minutes for me to make the usually fifteen-minute drive to the *mikvah*. The streets were icy and the snow was thick as I clutched the steering wheel with fright and *davened* to *Hashem* to carry us safely. While I drove, I chatted cheerily with my passenger so she wouldn't be nervous as we inched our way through the snow-covered streets.

"*Aibishter!* I'm doing this for you!" I thought as the car slid over icy patches and the engine revved through the heavy snow.

Boruch Hashem, we made it safely, and she *toiveled!* I drove her back home in our van.

By the end of the night there was over two feet of snow on the ground. The entire city was silent and white, and not a car moved until the plows came by later in the day. I marveled at how I had been able to get out and drive in the thick of the blizzard, and concluded that *Hashem* had cleared a path for me and Terry. For the *mikvah*, really.

A couple months later, Terry called.

"I'm expecting," she said, a smile in her voice. "I conceived the night of the snow storm."

She told me how scared she had been in the car that night, worried that we would get stuck or lost in the snow.

"You were so confident, and it calmed me so much," she told me, and it was my turn to smile silently on the other end.

I was so excited for her, and also so inspired by her commitment to *mikvah* and by her readiness to go outside of her comfort zone, despite the snow and her misgivings, to make it to the *mikvah* on time.

Story Forty-Two
Mikvah and OCD

Mikvah night. A night of reunion, connection, and joy. A night eagerly awaited with anticipation, the highlight of the month. Or at least that's how it's supposed to be.

But at the beginning of my marriage, I wasn't able to experience any of that. The beauty of this *mitzvah* was overshadowed by my anxiety. Month after month, my thoughts would overwhelm me.

On a regular day, I had no problem flossing my teeth in two minutes. For some reason, while preparing for *mikvah*, flossing was an incredibly daunting task. Flossing each tooth three times sounded like a good idea; all food was sure to be removed that way. But then the thoughts started crowding my mind.

Wait, what's that white stuff on the floss? Is it saliva or food? I can't tell. Better to err on the side of caution and floss that tooth three more times. One sec, did I miss a tooth? I'm not positive. Let me repeat this side. Better safe than sorry...

Forty-five minutes later, I'd finally put away the floss and move on to the next step of preparation, still uncertain that I actually removed all the food stuck in my teeth.

On to the makeup.

It's a total disaster! My eye makeup isn't coming off. My poor eyelids are burning from endless scrubbing. Let me just check again. Did I really completely remove all my makeup? Let me see...oh no! A small black smudge on the Q-tip! See? Good thing I double-checked.

Now for my nails...

By this point, I am a total wreck. The clock is oblivious, moving on as usual. I am trapped by my thoughts, choking up with tears and overcome with hopelessness. I am unable to slow my brain and move forward.

As I prepared, millions of questions popped up in my mind, and I sought reassurance from the *mikvah* lady. I made a mental note of all the issues as they came up. Though many of the questions were the exact same as the time before, I needed to ask them again.

When I finally left to go home, I hoped I could relax again until next month, but I had no peace. Inevitably, after every single *mikvah*, I was still under attack by my thoughts. Sometimes I thought of a *sha'aloh*[34] about my preparation immediately after I *toiveled*, sometimes it would come to me on the way home, and sometimes I found a question after I was home for a long while. They weren't real questions, just self-made doubts questioning my own actions, something else to obsess about and perpetuate the restlessness.

Considering how overwhelming it was for me, you may be shocked to hear that these days, my *mikvah* week is a calm week and *mikvah* day is calm like any other day. I plan a regular schedule and do everything as usual. In fact, with each day counted, my excitement for this *mitzvah* and reuniting with my husband grows; I look forward to going. There's nothing to be nervous about! It's a very spiritual experience for me. Now, I truly appreciate it.

What happened? What changed? How did *mikvah* become my favorite *mitzvah*?

Well, it took lots of hard work over a few years.

From the beginning, I instinctively knew that my process wasn't typical. After the third time I *toiveled* in the *mikvah*, I called my *kallah* teacher and described my general experience to her. She gave me many practical tips to help make my preparations faster and clarified what was necessary for me to do... and what wasn't. This insight made a huge difference. There were details that I had simply misunderstood, and I was just making it unnecessarily harder for myself.

My *kallah* teacher told me to check out a helpful chart from *mikvah.org* which outlines the approximate timing for every step of preparation. I was surprised how short the suggested times for all the

---

34 Question for a rabbi

preparations were! That didn't seem possible to me. I saw how my preparations were going way way over time! I wanted to resolve to stick to the recommended timing, but I felt there was no way I would be able to finish flossing in such a short amount of time; I thought I was always seeing more white things stuck between my teeth!

At the suggestion of my *kallah* teacher, I called a *Rav*. He confirmed that the timing was correct, and told me to work on my teeth just for the recommended five minutes. That phone call made a huge difference. Since then, I brush, floss, and rinse for five minutes, and then I calmly move on to the next step.

The eye make up removal was another huge issue. I came to realize there was a simple fix, and that was finding the right makeup remover! It took four tries, and lots of frustration, until I hit the jackpot. I finally found one that removes my makeup well, and together with my other efforts, I was able to finish removing my makeup faster.

I also got into the habit of making sure to be super busy the entire day of *mikvah* so I wouldn't have any time to think. I forced myself to replace my anxious thoughts with positive thoughts, and to pretend I was calm, even if I didn't feel so. It worked. I was still anxious, but acting as if I wasn't, quieted a lot of the jitters. The next month, I worked hard both at remaining calm and sticking to the proper time frame. After another five months of persevering, I reached a point where my anxiety during preparations was at a minimum. My preparation was done in a calm manner and in a very decent amount of time. It wasn't perfect, but I kept on seeing improvement.

Once my anxious thoughts were relegated to the back of my mind, I was able to focus on appreciating the *mikvah*. I would eagerly count my days excitedly anticipating reuniting with my husband.

***

After a few months of calm preparations, my questions *after* I returned from the *mikvah* were not going away. I decided to give therapy an honest try. I learnt that getting reassurance from a *mikvah* lady, *Rav*, *kallah* teacher, or even myself, was a compulsion, and those questions were considered obsessive thoughts. The more I gave in to the compulsions, the more the obsessive thoughts would grow and become more powerful. They would just keep getting stronger and stronger, coming back to bother me. What an eye-opener!

I began to change the way that I prepared for *mikvah*: I wrote myself a very detailed preparation checklist and laminated the list so it would be waterproof. When I prepared for *mikvah*, I put a sticker over each step as soon as I completed it. "Remove makeup" was broken up as remove eyeliner, remove eye shadow, remove lipstick, remove blush from cheeks, etc.

When I went into the *mikvah*, I could prove to myself I had completed all my preparations properly, because my chart was covered with stickers. After I came out, if I had any question, I would ask myself, "Did I skip a step of preparing? Nope. Not even possible. I already put a sticker on every step on my chart."

But those "what if" questions were still bombarding me after *mikvah*. My therapist suggested I call another *Rav* who had experience with OCD and explain that after every *mikvah* I have so many "what if" questions. The *Rav* said that since these questions come from anxiety, I don't have to worry about them. Any question with the key words "what if," "maybe", "I think," "I don't remember," is coming from anxiety. The *Rav* said if I have an "anxiety question," I should not pay attention to it, just push the doubt away. I should not allow those thoughts to overtake my mind and stop me from fulfilling this special *mitzvah*. I breathed a sigh of relief and realized those were imaginary burdens on my shoulders. My thoughts were clearly coming from anxiety and I didn't need to worry about them.

(*If you are having obsessive thoughts, you must call a Rav and ask your own question. If they persist, then seek the professional guidance of a mental health specialist. – Ed.*)

The next month, I was very hopeful. I was finally prepared for battle. When a question came to me, I put it through a filter, "Is there an anxiety key word in my question?" Yes! Well then, it's anxiety, and I would push it away without thinking about it. Every time the question tried coming back to bother me, I would just say to myself, "It's just a thought." Did I skip a step of preparing? Nope. Not even possible. I already put a sticker on every step on my chart. I also acted calm, although inside I was extremely tense. Somehow that fake face helped. Over time, the thoughts became quieter and quieter.

A lot also changed when I realized that these overwhelming thoughts that I had were actually a challenge that *Hashem* had given me. Some people have challenges going to *mikvah* because they live far away from one or because they have medical issues. *Hashem* gave me the challenge of Obsessive Compulsion, and He also gave me the strength to overcome it. My mission is replacing my anxious thoughts so I experience the beauty of going to *mikvah*.

After a journey of three years, nowadays, preparing takes me a reasonable amount of time. I just do what I'm supposed to do, once, and move on. The voices planting doubts are so weak and flimsy, I just completely ignore them. I don't ask "what if" questions after I *toivel*. I just don't have any of those sorts of questions anymore! The slip-ups happen much more rarely, and I am confident that things will get even better.

I have no way of knowing if I will ever be "cured." At any point the OCD might creep back, but I am prepared for that. I'll occasionally repeat something as I'm preparing, just to relieve the obsession. Sometimes, I'll be SO tempted...but I won't. Instead, I send those thoughts flying so fast they don't know what hit them. I know exactly what the thoughts are, and how to handle them. I'm stronger than them. I am at peace with my struggle and now I look forward to going to *mikvah*. I have become stronger and more connected to *Hashem* because of this challenge, and it makes *mikvah* that much more meaningful. My journey has made this beautiful *mitzvah* an exciting opportunity to treasure.

(Note: This story is one woman's story and does not reflect the experiences of all women with OCD. OCD can be pretty common but affects each person in different ways – from mild to severe and in different types of thoughts. See appendix for more information on mikvah and OCD)

Story Forty-Three
Mikvah During the COVID-19 Pandemic. One

Here in our country, south of the equator, we were in the winter season when COVID-19 arrived. The government hit us hard with some of the most stringent COVID-19 rules on the planet, and they were not very forgiving of religious observance. Unlike other places which allowed permits or other leniencies, the police here were very strict. A mother was fined over $1600 for giving her daughter driving lessons, and the authorities threatened that anyone caught merely drinking a coffee on a bench could be fined $1000 and spend up to six months in jail. There was also a curfew in effect from 8:00 P.M. until 5:00 A.M. that lasted for three months.

Under these conditions, we utilized the strictest standards for COVID-free cleaning in our *mikvah*. Women did their preparations at home and were only allowed one at a time in the building. I wore gloves and masks and we put extra chlorine in the water. However, the government did not consider using the *mikvah* an "essential service."

Luckily, the curfew was implemented during our winter, and women were able to come *toivel* before the curfew. This wasn't easy by any means because people were only allowed to be out for essential reasons. The women had to sneak out and hope that they wouldn't get ticketed.

As the days started to get longer again, there was a pressing concern. How would women be able to get to *mikvah* once the clocks changed and the time for *tevilah* would be during the curfew?

It was super scary, and it would have been extremely complicated. *Baruch Hashem*, in what could only be described as a miracle, the curfew was lifted the night before daylight savings started and our late summer hours began! *Hashem* was looking out for us!

Story Forty-Four
Mikvah During the COVID-19 Pandemic. Two

Going to *mikvah* during the lock-down period of the COVID-19 pandemic wasn't an easy feat for many women, especially at the beginning of the pandemic. Although immersion in the *mikvah* is not a source of Covid-19 transmission, there were several countries that had extreme lock-down rules and even nightly curfews. Some women in remote places had to use the ocean or speed up the building of their own *mikvahs*. Some women were able to bribe the policemen in their country, while other women went to secret *mikvahs*.

In the country where I live, they closed the domestic borders, meaning I couldn't go from one state to the other. I couldn't drive anywhere and there were no flights for eight months. This was very difficult for me, because I live in a remote city and I am used to driving several hours to use the *mikvah*. Now there were no options! The ocean was "closed", and I couldn't get to the *mikvah*.

To make it worse, our government announced a strict curfew. No one could leave their houses from 7:00 P.M. until 5:00 A.M. Even during the day, there were stringent rules. Men could leave their houses for two hours at a time, but only on Tuesdays and Thursdays. Women were a little luckier because they were allowed out three times a week: Monday, Wednesday, and Friday, depending on the last digits of their government issued ID. On weekends, everyone had to stay home.

My *mikvah* night fell three days after everything was shut down. My husband and I felt so insecure. We had no idea how I would make it to the *mikvah*.

Out of the blue, a neighbor came by to talk to us. He was an American doctor and was well connected to all the right people in town. He mentioned to my husband that he had a contact with the mayor, and he could get us a permit if we needed to travel. This was *mamesh* a miracle from heaven, because at that time, no one was given permission to travel around.

We felt so relieved and grateful to *Hashem* for arranging this for us. We could see how *Hashem* was pulling the strings to make sure I was able to use the *mikvah*!

It was a life lesson. All over the world, anything deemed "unessential" was closed. In the Jewish communities, *shuls* were closed, men didn't hear the Torah read, or gather in a *minyan*. Schools may have been open online, but it was up to the parents to make sure their children were learning. The only public Jewish institution that never shut down was the women's *mikvah*. All over the world, women had to do things they'd never dreamed of to get to the *mikvah*.

In a time when women may sometimes feel that the *shul* or school is the place where all of *Yiddishkeit* happens, and what goes on in the home is of no importance, COVID-19 drove home the opposite point. It powerfully illustrated how Jewish life and continuity could carry on when *shuls* were closed, but could not continue without the Jewish home; the *mitzvos* of *Shabbos*, *Kashrus* and *Taharas Hamishpacha*.

As the *Akeres HaBayis*[35], it is the woman who is entrusted with the *mitzvos* of *Shabbos*, *Kashrus*, and *Taharas Hamishpacha* in her home. A woman's word is implicitly believed in these areas (there's no *mashgiach* in her kitchen!) because she has the primary responsibility of raising her children with Torah values and infusing them with love for Torah and *mitzvos*. As much as a child receives from *shul* and school, the values received from home run deepest. The continuity of the Jewish people, i.e. having Jewish children and raising them Jewish, is dependent on the Jewish mother and the Jewish home. That is why, when everything else was closed, women's *mikvahs* were open.

---

35 This refers to the concept that a Jewish woman is the foundation of her family and is the primary driver of the environment in the home.

Story Forty-Five
Mikvah During the COVID-19 Pandemic. Three

When we first moved to the remote island where we live, the mitzvah of *mikvah* presented a challenge. Our island is located a few hours' flight away from the nearest *frum* communities. This meant a couple hundred dollars a month, a new excuse for the kids every four weeks ("You're traveling again? Didn't we just get milk a month ago?!"), and arranging all of the logistics of the journey, both for myself and for my family staying behind. When my *mikvah* night fell on *Shabbos* or *Yom Tov*, I would make arrangements to travel to the *frum* communities.

Once during a three-day *Yom Tov*, I had to stay home and *toivel* in a freezing river and I turned to my husband and announced, "That's it. I'm never doing that again." I'm not an adventurous person by any means, and let me tell you, I was not thrilled to be roughing it in natural waters. I like my warm bath, my spa atmosphere, and the opportunity to pamper myself a bit. The river was definitely not my cup of tea.

But 'never again' is a long time, and in March of 2020 Covid-19 took over the world, and our island locked down its borders essentially cutting us off from the rest of the country. It was practically impossible for anyone to fly out and extremely difficult to fly in to the mainland as well. With my *mikvah* night fast approaching, I realized that I would have to eat my words and *toivel* here. And it wasn't even

Shabbos! We spoke with our *Rav* and weighed our options, and finally decided on a beach about an hour drive away.

My heart was in my throat the entire hour. I don't know if I was more scared of the cold or of being stopped by police and having to explain to them what we were doing at the beach in the middle of a pandemic. I imagined the ridiculous scene over and over.

Me: "Oh officer, we were just going to have a dunk!"

Officer: "In the middle of the night?! In the middle of a lock-down?!"

I was absolutely mortified just thinking about it.

"This is just not a viable long-term plan." I said to my husband on the way back home (having thankfully not met my imagined officer, but still...) "We need a proper *mikvah* here."

We knew about an old, unused *mikvah* in a city about two- and-a -half hours away from where we live, which had been built many years ago and was decaying, but in the middle of the pandemic lock-down, it looked like our best option. My husband began to make weekly trips there to evaluate and work on the *mikvah*, speaking with *Rabbonim* and experts from around the world. Each week brought new problems needing solutions that were not always easy to come by, but we persevered, and after a few weeks of working on fixing the various *halachic* issues, my husband announced that the *mikvah* was ready to be cleaned and filled.

He spent hours scrubbing the walls of the *bor* and the preparation rooms of the *mikvah* which hadn't been used in over 20 years, and then hours more transporting over 300 blocks of ice to fill the *bor*. After days of preparation, everything seemed ready. All we had to do was wait for the ice to melt and the *mikvah* would be up and running. We finally had a (semi-)local *mikvah*!

Little did we know that 300 blocks of ice do not melt very quickly. The wait was excruciating. After all the work we had done and knowing that we had a real, kosher *mikvah*, we still had to wait about a week for the *mikvah* to be fully operational.

When it finally did melt, the *simcha* we felt was unparalleled. Now we really had a *mikvah*!

Story Forty-Six
Mikvah During the COVID-19 Pandemic. Four

Until 2020, we thought that the days of sneaking to *mikvah* in the dead of the night were left behind with the fall of the Soviet Union. Then the COVID-19 pandemic came to our city.

Every country has a different culture. The culture in my country is that people follow the rules. If there is a curfew from 8:00 P.M to 5:00 A.M., then you stay home from 8:00 P.M to 5:00 A.M. . Anyone who broke the rules was slapped with a fine from one to six-thousand dollars(!) from the many police milling around waiting to pounce.

On top of that, the local government purposely and infuriatingly shut down the women's *mikvahs*. Policemen were stationed outside to make sure no one went in.

We were all scared.

We had never lived through something like this before. Walking outside was enough reason for a massive fine. Would we be taken to jail?

We were told it would be for a month, but it just kept going on and on.

Yet, the heroic women in charge of the *mikvahs* made sure every woman was able to use the *mikvah*. Equally heroic were the women that had to brave the scary unknown, furtively walking to *mikvah* while *davening* that no one should see them.

Even more remarkable, is how we grew up in an environment where there was very little government intervention in the performance of *mitzvos*. It's not as though we were born in Communist Russia where going undercover would be ingrained in us with our mother's milk. Although it was completely foreign for us to sneak to *mikvah* risking staggering fines, we did it anyway, because there is no power on earth that can stop Jewish continuity.

Story Forty-Seven
Real Women, Real Mesiras Nefesh

Women face all kinds of challenges in their fulfillment of the *mitzvah* of *Taharas Hamishpacha*, but I will never forget the time when Lauren* came to *toivel* during the Corona lock-down.

Lauren lives about an hour away from my city, up in the countryside mountains. I've always respected Lauren as a sincere, beautiful woman who takes her *Yiddishkeit* very seriously. Usually, Lauren uses the *mikvah* in her area, but the *mikvah* was closed because of the lock-down.

Not to be deterred, she called me for an appointment. Little did I know that Lauren was driving an old, battered car that really was not suited for the drive through the mountains. The car overheated on the way and refused to budge. Ever the optimist, Lauren called her mechanic to figure out what to do. Luckily, the mechanic was able to explain what needed to be done and she eventually made it.

The story was not over when she got here, because she still had to wait for her car to cool down before she could leave! We had a remarkable talk and although I thought I was going to encourage her, she ended up inspiring me!

You know, there are really so many incredible women with such real *mesiras nefesh* for *mikvah*.

Mikvah-Related OCD and How to Help

Reviewed by Dr. Yael Mayefsky, PhD,
Licensed Clinical Psychologist

What is OCD?

Obsessive Compulsive Disorder (OCD) is a disorder of the mind that causes a person to have repetitive unwanted thoughts (obsessions) or behaviors (compulsions). Symptoms can vary from mild to severe and they have varying effects on everyday living.

Obsessions are:

1. Recurrent unwanted thoughts and urges that in most individuals cause anxiety or distress.

AND 2. The individual attempts to suppress such thoughts with some other thought or action (i.e., by performing a compulsion).

Compulsions are:

1. Mental acts or repetitive behaviors (like hand washing or checking) that the individual feels driven to perform.

AND 2. The behaviors or mental acts will not realistically prevent the anxiety/dreaded event or are clearly excessive.

Most people with OCD know that the behaviors do not make sense, but they cannot stop themselves from repeating them. Of course, people with OCD do not want these thoughts or behaviors to control them, and they find them disturbing. For some, the thoughts occur only once in a while and are mildly annoying. For others, the thoughts are constant and affect their ability to live their life. The behaviors tend to make them nervous and afraid of their lack of control.

OCD is common, affecting about 1 in 40 people and can run in families. There are also many common OCD thoughts. One is fear of germs: those with this compulsion can be found repeatedly washing their hands. Through repetitive washing, they find temporary relief from the anxiety of contact with germs, but soon afterward the nervousness returns and they find themselves back once again at the sink, in yet another attempt to find some relief. There are also typical OCD behaviors that involve religious rituals. For example, a homemaker might obsess about milk touching meat products or dishes. On *Pesach*, one might fear that all *chametz* (leaven) has not been thoroughly removed. There is fear of *tumah* (impurity) in the negel vasser (hand-washing) basin, so the individual will wash and rewash.

Then there is the woman with *mikvah* OCD. Many *frum* (observant) women may not know they have this disorder. Because of their lack of awareness, these women have no clue that what they are suffering is a medically classified DSM (Diagnostic and Statistical Manual) disorder. Most of the time they usually function without compulsive thoughts; however, in the area of ritual (and for some, in more than one area), their brains go haywire. OCD is what this author's Psych 101 professor called a broken-pocketed brain syndrome — meaning all other parts of the brain seem to work, except for this one part.

While to an outsider a woman preparing herself for the *mikvah* might be praised for being extra-scrupulous, the woman with OCD is operating in a different orbit. In an extreme case of OCD, the scenario goes like this: First, the woman (call her Malkie) spends 10-15 minutes, twice a day, checking her *bedika* (white) cloths. She keeps asking herself, "Did I cover all areas? Are the *bedika* cloths completely white? Can I start counting? Did I check in the correct lighting?" During the few days before immersion, she begins the process. She then has the nagging thought that she did not sufficiently clean a particular part of her body. So, she then cleans herself over and over again until she has scrubbed herself raw. Malkie checks the next area, her teeth. For over a half hour she continues flossing until her gums start to bleed. She cuts her nails all the way below the nail line until her fingers hurt, and then she removes the cuticles until they start to bleed as well. The preparation process is a living hell for these women. The agony they go through is unimaginable. Dinner is not cooked, laundry not folded — the to-do list never becomes marked off as "done" — because all Malkie has been doing the whole day is getting ready for the *mikvah*.

The minute the *mikvah* opens up, she is there, and she is the last to leave — way past the time the *mikvah* was supposed to close. The hour is midnight. While in the *mikvah*, she is super-stressed, since other women are waiting and the *mikvah* lady is even knocking on her door to see if everything is okay. Alone and embarrassed, Malkie is on the verge of tears and questions herself, "What's wrong with me? Why am I not managing like other women?" She cries from deep within. "Help! Help! I need to finish and get going!" When she is finally done and ready to immerse, she breaks out in a cold sweat and wonders, "Did I do the proper *bedika*? Did I check enough, and scrub enough?" Even her red, raw skin does not convince her she did it right. She immerses with doubts and concerns and feels terrible that she has inadvertently caused the *mikvah* attendant to stay late, while her husband is waiting at home for her. Coming home, she is nervous once again. She tells her husband who unsuccessfully tries to convince her that everything is fine.

Her obsessive thoughts creep up, making her feel too non-kosher to be intimate with him. She panics and wants to call the *Rav* again. Yes, again. So, she phones the *Rav*, who reassures her that after the fact, even if she did not scrub an area of her thigh, the tevilah is still kosher. She explains several times, and the *Rav* reassures her again and again. As Malkie hangs up the phone, she broods, "Did I explain myself clearly to the *Rav*? Did I give him all the details?" Now it is 1:00 A.M, and she is exhausted. Her husband at this point may think, "What is wrong? Is this what every man goes through with his wife? Is this what G-d has intended"? No one has ever prepared him for this!

Unfortunately, the turmoil has just begun. Now Malkie wonders if she has caused her husband to sin by having relations with her when she may have not have properly prepared for her immersion. If she has conceived, she wonders whether the new baby will be "kosher." Every day she worries; every day she panics. She wants to get pregnant, but then again she hopes she does not, because of her fear of having created an "impure" baby. Then the day comes, and she finds out she is pregnant. She has mixed feelings, mostly not good feelings. If she miscarries, she feels relieved because of her doubts. However, that is still not the end of it. In another few weeks, she has to return again."

Adapted from "Heavenly Waters" by Miriam Yerushalmi

What Can Be Done?

The good news is that these thoughts can be managed. The right management will depend on the type of symptoms.

When it comes to obsessive thoughts and *mikvah*, for a woman with mild symptoms it can be helpful to:

A.   Review the *halachos*, laws, with your *kallah* teacher/*mikvah* attendant / *Rebbetzin* and know what actually needs to be cleaned and how extensively.

B.   Use a chart with suggested times, to see if you're spending too much time in any one area (see www.*mikvah*.org for a special *mikvah* and OCD preparation checklist).

C.   Have a thorough conversation with a *Rav* to understand when and what is an issue after immersion if one fears she forgot something. More often than not, it is not necessary to re-immerse. However gaining clarity and knowing when it is safe to assume everything was done properly can ease tension and stress.

D.   Remember that *Hashem* doesn't expect you to be perfect, just to try your best.

What about when that's not enough?

How to Know When to Get Help:

A good rule to keep in mind when deciding when to get help for any difficulty is to see how much the difficulty is affecting your life. Check the duration (how long it lasts), the frequency (how often it happens) and the intensity (mild to severe) of the behavior that you are worried about.

If anxious or obsessive thoughts are affecting your ability to leave the *mikvah* happily and at peace, especially for more than three months in a row, then it's time to get help.

There are several types of treatment options available. For moderate cases, symptoms mostly resolve with several months to years of therapy (specifically, Cognitive Behavioral Therapy with ERP, or Exposure and Response Prevention). There is also a program called the "*Taharas HaMishpacha Workbook*" which is a detailed guide for overcoming *mikvah*-related OCD. (See the "Resources" in the back of this book for more information.)

With *Hashem*'s help, there are therapies and treatments available to overcome OCD. There are also therapists and Psychologists who specialize in OCD and *mikvah*. Getting help is an investment in yourself, your husband, your marriage and your relationship with *Hashem*. May all those who struggle with this be successful and have beautiful, stress-free preparations for *mikvah*.

Resources

Further Reading:

Family Purity (2000) by Rabbi Fishel Jacobs

An in-depth guide to the laws of Taharas Hamishpacha for beginners and non-beginners alike. Recommended in conjunction with guidance from an Orthodox Rabbi/Rebbetzin

Total Immersion (Revised 2006) by Mrs. Rivkah Slonim

An anthology of fifty essays and stories collecting thoughts about mikvah from varied lenses.

www.mikvah.org

A comprehensive website with lectures and articles, interactive mikvah calendar app, resources, mikvah directory and a whole host of other features.

Shall We Have Another? (2019) by Rabbi Mendel Dubov

An in-depth look at family planning from a Torah perspective

The Taharas Hamishpacha Workbook: A Program for Overcoming Mikvah-Related Anxiety (2017) by Rabbi David Kaufman

This workbook is a valuable resource for women suffering from anxiety or OCD (Obsessive-Compulsive Disorder) particularly regarding Taharas Hamishpacha (family purity), mikvah, and related issues.

It is not a guide to the halachos (laws) of Taharas Hamishpacha. Rather, it enables a woman who has anxiety regarding these matters overcome her anxiety, by guiding her through an evidence-based step-by-step program using proven cognitive-behavioral therapy techniques. It can be used as a self-help book or as a treatment manual in a therapy setting.

The book teaches how to deal with uncertainty, fear of taking risks, and extreme fear of sinning. It addresses how women can learn to face these challenges without compromising on their Jewish values. And to the contrary, how Jewish values encourage living with joy and happiness rather than anxiety and fear.

It teaches how to learn to take risks, how to identify feared consequences, and how to set up an exposure hierarchy. It also teaches bossing back techniques and what to do (and not to do) about obsessions in general, and specifically before and after tevilah. The book includes reproducible worksheets and mikvah preparation timetables.

Glossary

These explanations are given in context of the book and are not exact translations. Some words have multiple meanings that are not expounded on here.

Acharon Shel Pesach: The last day of Passover

Ad Kan: That's it! No more!

Ahavas Hashem: A deep all-encompassing love of G-d

Aibershter: The Yiddish word for G-d, This expression is often used in a moment of difficulty and evokes a child calling to their parent.

Akeres Habayis: Lit. "Foundation of the home." This refers to the concept that a Jewish woman is the bedrock of her family and is the primary driver of the environment in the home

Bais Yaacov: An Orthodox Jewish school for girls

Baruch Hashem: Thank G-d! or Praise G-d!

Bashert: Soulmate

Bedikah: One of the steps of the process of becoming *Tehora*

Beis Hamikdash: Holy Temple

Bitachon: Absolute belief in G-d

Bochen klayos valev: Lit. "Checking hearts and minds." This refers to G-d knowing the struggles, thoughts and feelings of each of us

Bochurim: Yeshiva students

Bor: Every mikvah pool is connected to a bor (usually a cement cistern) which needs to be filled with pure rainwater. The mikvah pool is connected to this bor and is filled with regular water which is changed and filtered as needed

Bracha, brachos: Blessing, blessings

B'shaa tova: Lit. "In a good hour". This is a customary greeting to a woman who is pregnant, wishing her an easy birth, at the right time.

B'tahara: In purity

Chabad House: A place for one's weary neshamah to find a home. A place where one can connect to their Jewish roots and come closer to G-d.

Chafifah: Cleaning the body before immersing

Chamudee: A term of endearment in Hebrew for "cutie"

Chatzitzah: Lit. "An obstruction." When immersing in the mikvah, there may not be anything extra on the body that can obstruct the mikvah waters from flowing and touching the entire person.

Chizuk: Empowerment

Chuppah: Marriage ceremony

Daven, davening: Pray

Emunah: Faith in G-d

Eretz Yisroel: Land of Israel

Farbrengen: Chassidic gathering of inspiration and soul-stirring

Frum: Orthodox Jewish

Gadol, Gedolim: A leading Torah scholar/s

Halacha: Jewish law

Hashem: G-d

Hashgacha pratis: Lit. "Every single piece of this world; including every action, every thought, every person, every leaf that blows has been preordained by G-d." Used in the book to point out how random events that seem to be coincidental have clearly been orchestrated by G-d

Hayom Yom: A book of daily Torah thoughts

Hefsek taharah: The first step in becoming *Tehorah*

Hidur mitzvah: Lit. "To beautify a *mitzvah*". This means to put extra effort into the fulfillment of a *mitzvah*

K'rtzon Avinu Shebashamayim: Lit. "According to the will of our Father in Heaven"

Kallah: Bride

Keine ayin hara: A Yiddish expression for warding off the 'evil eye'

Kiddush: In the context of this story, this refers to a celebration in the synagouge after praying, to celebrate the birth of a daughter

Klipah: Negative energy

Kvetch: Complaining

Lubavitcher Rebbe: Rabbi Menachem Mendel Schneerson, Leader of the Chabad-Lubavitch movement

Maariv: Evening prayer

Malach: Hebrew for angel, messenger

Mashgiach: Someone who supervises food production to ensure that it is *kosher*

Mashpia: Jewish spiritual mentor, Someone who guides in religious matters and its effects on everyday life.

Mesiras nefesh: Lit. "Self- sacrifice." Referring to all the big and small sacrifices we make, from giving up creature comforts to risk-taking, in order to do G-d's will.

Mikvah: Lit. "The holy waters in which men or women immerse to become pure." Also refers to the overall experiences and laws that a woman follows in order to become pure.

Mitzrayim: Egypt during the time of our slavery as mentioned in the Passover story

Mitzvah: An instruction given to us by G-d that allows us to relate to and connect to his Omnipresence.

Moshiach: The future redeemer who will take us out of exile, rebuild the Holy Temple and bring peace to the world.

Motzai Shabbos: Saturday night

Motzei Yom Kippur: After Yom Kippur ends

Nachas: An overflowing pride usually from one's children or grandchildren that often starts in the heart and swells to the head and feet

Neshamah: The soul; an actual part of G-d himself that he placed into each of us, the part of us that is connected to him no matter what, the part of us that pulls us to do Jewish.

Niddah: Lit. "Separation." This can mean many things. It can refer to menstruation. It can refer to the period from when a woman becomes impure through the laws of becoming niddah (beyond the scope of this book) until she has properly immersed in the mikvah. In the book, this also refers to the that time of the month when we are reminded of our feminine powers, a monthly reminder of the gift of the possibility of creating life and often a time when we discover our inner strength through hard moments.

Nuuu?: And so....?

Ob"m: Of blessed memory

Pesach: Passover

Poskim: Great Rabbonim of yesteryear who have decided matters of Jewish law

Rabbanit: Variation of Rebbetzin (see below)

Rabbonim: Plural of Rav (see below)

Rashi: A Torah Scholar of the twelfth century who explained Chumash and Gemara in a manner that is easy to understand.

Rav: A Rabbi who answers questions on Jewish law

Rebbetzin: Rabbi's wife, Female scholar, A wise, older women who is knowledgeable in the Torah and womanly matters and guides others accordingly.

Rivka Immainu: Rebecca of the Bible

Rosh Chodesh Adar: The first day of the Jewish month of Adar, the month of Purim.

Rosh Yeshiva: An extremely learned person who is responsible for guiding, teaching and educating yeshiva students of all ages.

Sara Immainu: Sarah of the Bible

Sephardim: This commonly refers to Jews of Middle Eastern or North African origin or those that follow the Sephardic tradition

Sefer: Jewish holy book

Segulot v'Matanot!: Hebrew for rituals and gifts

Shabbos: Shabbat

Shailoh: Question

Shavua Tov: The customary greeting after Shabbat in which one wishes the other a good week

Shechina: Divine Prescence

Sheva minim: The seven special fruits of the Land of Israel listed in the Torah

Shlucha: Wife, mother, Rebbetzin, cook, shepherd of souls. The definition may change daily, weekly, hourly. A woman who has made it her life's mission to be there for others; spiritually, religiously and practically.

Sholom bayis: Literally, "peace in the home". This common phrase is used in many different contexts to refer to a harmonious, loving relationship between husband and wife.

Shomer Shabbat: Someone who keeps the laws of Shabbat

Shul: Synagogue

Shvigger: Mother-in-law

Siddur: Prayer book

Sifrei Torah: Torah scrolls

Sifsei Chachamim: A commentator on the Torah

Simchah: Hebrew for celebration

Tahara: Lit. "A state of purity." This refers to an intimate level of connection to G-d that requires preparation, including immersing in the mikvah

Taharas Hamishpacha: Literally "Laws of family purity". This refers to the collection of laws regarding marriage, intimacy, preparing for and using the mikvah.

Tefillah: Prayer

Tehillim: Psalms

Tehora: Pure, see *Tahara*

Tevilah: Immersion

Tichel: A scarf or snood or other similar hair covering worn by married women to keep their hair private. Covering one's hair after marriage brings blessings to the marriage and children.

Toivel: The act of immersing

Tzedakah: Lit. Justice. This is colloquially used to refer to organizations that help others because in a just world, we share what we have with others.

Yaharog v'al yavor: A person should let themselves be killed rather than transgress a specific mitzvah

Yehupitz: The middle of nowhere

Yeshuos: Extraordinary help from G-d

Yetzer Hora: Evil inclination, the voice inside that encourages one to do the wrong thing

Yiddishe nachas: A pride that results from Jewish behavior.

Yiddishe neshama: A Jewish soul

Yiddishkeit: All-encompassing Jewishness

Yiras Shomayim: Deep fear of Heaven that permeates one's thoughts, speech and actions

Ym"sm: Yemach Shemom- May their names be erased. An expression used when mentioning evil people.

Yom Tov: Festival

Zchus: A privilege or an honor

Biography

Chaya Raichik lives with her husband and children in Brooklyn, NY. After her marriage, she was perusing the shelves of local Judaica stores and noticed a lack of modern-day, inspirational mikvah stories. This led to the creation of Mikvah Stories. Chaya is a teacher and educator and enjoys helping students of all ages channel their inner potential to achieve real growth by connecting to them as they are and encouraging them to strive higher. She is passionate about all things Torah and Woman. She believes in empowering girls and women to embrace, appreciate and cherish their space in Judaism. Additionally, she advocates for womens' needs and for the inclusion, acceptance and love of all of G-d's children.